How to Handle Trouble

How to Handle Trouble

JOHN CARMODY

DOUBLEDAY

NEW YORK   LONDON   TORONTO

SYDNEY   AUCKLAND

PUBLISHED BY DOUBLEDAY
a division of Bantam Doubleday Dell Publishing Group, Inc.
1540 Broadway, New York, New York 10036

DOUBLEDAY and the portrayal of an anchor with a dolphin are
trademarks of Doubleday, a division of Bantam Doubleday
Dell Publishing Group, Inc.

DESIGN BY GLEN M. EDELSTEIN

LIBRARY OF CONGRESS CATALOGING-IN-PUBLICATION DATA

CARMODY, JOHN, 1939–
    HOW TO HANDLE TROUBLE / JOHN CARMODY. — 1ST ED.
        P.   CM.
    INCLUDES BIBLIOGRAPHICAL REFERENCES.
    1. SUFFERING—RELIGIOUS ASPECTS.   2. CONSOLATION.
    I. TITLE.
BL65.S85C37   1993
248.8´6—DC20   93-16848
                                                    CIP

ISBN 0-385-47120-3

PRINTED IN THE UNITED STATES OF AMERICA
OCTOBER 1993
FIRST EDITION

10   9   8   7   6   5   4   3   2   1

For Richard Watt, M.D.

Contents

Introduction

THIS BOOK IS FOR PEOPLE IN TROUBLE. YOU know who you are. You have a problem. You feel a pain. Your life is not what you'd like it to be and you need help. I want to offer you help, but not as though standing apart, like one who has no troubles. I want to offer you the help of a fellow sufferer. What I have to say comes from pain I myself have yet to overcome.

My trouble is bone cancer. In mid-April of 1992 I was diagnosed as having a moderately advanced case of multiple myeloma. This disease is incurable. From diagnosis to death, the average time of survival is three years. Multiple myeloma has broken my back, put me in the hospital for a month, necessitated an operation to insert a two-foot titanium rod in my right leg, and sometimes caused me excruciating pain. It has also assaulted my spirit. On dark days, such as those when the withdrawal of drugs used in chemotherapy has left me aching in every bone like a reforming addict, I have said to my God, "You do terrible things to your people." I have dreamed of ancient Mexican gods lapping up human blood. I have wept at the pain I am causing my wife and others who love me. And I have felt unbearably lonely.

Still, I have learned that there are ways to handle trouble. There are ways to think and feel that lessen its pains. Just as deep breathing can sometimes relieve physical pain, so reflection, cultivating joy, and opening one's heart to good friends can sometimes lessen confusion or sorrow or loneliness. Real troubles seldom vanish completely. Multiple myeloma rarely stays in full remission. But day by day we can win significant victories over our troubles. With a little planning, a little courage, a little faith, we can regain the feeling that our life lies in our hands. Trouble can make us feel we have lost control of our life. The techniques I propose here can help us feel we have taken control back.

TECHNIQUES

"Techniques" is a contemporary word. I use it because it is fashionable. Everywhere people want to know how to do something. To get ahead, it is crucial to master computers, or persuasive speaking, or financial planning. My techniques, however, are really old-fashioned. I am more interested in helping you learn how to become something than how to do something. My concern is more with your self than with your machines or your speech or your money. For I believe that if you understand how you think and feel, you have a shot at wisdom. If you know how to bare your soul and take charge of your fate, you have a shot at conquering your trouble. Finally, if you know how to pray—contemplate the mysteriousness we can never remove from our lives—you have a shot at gaining deep peace.

The old-fashioned techniques for approaching wisdom, the conquest of trouble, and deep peace are very simple. They require time, but little space. They are not expensive and do not come packaged as software. If at first they seem demanding, because unfamiliar, soon they become not just familiar but pleasing. For they boil down to exercising the contemplative parts of our selves, which standard American culture has left flabby. As soon as we learn to think reflectively, guide our emotions, and disclose what's in our hearts to trustworthy listeners, we're on the path to significant satisfaction. We find it more and more natural to examine our experience, draw close to our feelings, and tell a few other people what is going on inside us. Equally, we find it more and more natural to decide what course of action we ought to take, and then to abandon our fate to the mystery that billions of people call God. So learning the basic ways of the contemplative life is often like coming home. We were lost and did not even know it. Now we are becoming found, and it feels wonderful.

The source of my techniques is the mainstream traditions of wisdom, West and East, that have nourished human beings since the dawn of human history. Much of what I shall suggest for handling trouble has been elaborated by shamans and yogis, mystics and priests. My version, though, is not elaborate. It is not secret or hidden or available only to a gifted few. It comes like a warranty with your basic human equipment. If you have a mind and a heart, you are a good candidate. As soon as you want to handle your trouble—as soon as you long to gain some control over your pain—you are asking for this wisdom. Twenty-five hundred years ago you might have gone to the Buddha for a good version. Two thousand years ago you might have gone to Jesus. Many Hindus and Chinese, Muslims and Jews, have been expert in this wisdom. Many Native Americans, Native Africans, and Native Australians have guided their lives by it.

MYSTERY

We need contemplative techniques, elaborate or simple, because the meaning of our lives is not apparent. The paradoxical blessing of getting into trouble is that trouble forces us to face this bedrock fact. As long as our lives are moving along easily, successfully, we can think that they make great sense. In fact, little about us human beings makes any sense. Where did we come from? What caused the big bang? Where are we going? What happens at death? We cannot answer any of these elementary questions with certitude. No human being on earth can guarantee what a man or woman is worth, or say definitively how a man or woman ought to live. This strange fundamental reality is as amusing as it is frightening. That everything truly significant about any man or woman is mysterious means that every honest person begins by confessing a great ignorance and so, ideally, a great humility.

What does my multiple myeloma mean? Can any of you tell me with certainty? Have I been cursed by God or blessed? Can you guarantee there is a God who curses or blesses? Can you be sure there is not such a God? All of these questions are beyond you, as they are beyond me and every other human being. If we have strong opinions about them, those opinions come from faith—some more-than-rational stance we've taken toward the mysteriousness of all human life.

I want to make this mysteriousness your friend. If I can, you will be well launched on the contemplative path, and thus well on your way to getting what handle human beings can on their worse troubles. Our worst troubles are those that make it difficult for us to see how we ought to proceed, what we ought to do, whether we can still think it good we were born. For example, if we are alcoholic, or someone crucial in our family is, and we have not come to grips with this fact, our lives are bound to be chaotic. We have no control over our drinking, and so we strew ruin left and right. That was the case in the household where I grew up. My father's alcoholism was the first big trouble with which I had to contend. Because I did contend with it, for years and years, I was somewhat prepared when bone cancer blew in. I had already swum in dark currents. Being plunged back in by cancer was horrible, but at least I had a serviceable swimming stroke.

There is a sameness in serious troubles. Alcoholism is different from cancer, as it is different from addiction to cocaine, but not completely so. Even if one trouble seems to be of our own making while another comes to us from outside, our being troubled is similar in both cases. We have problems to solve, so we need to get our heads straight. We have physical and spiritual pains to manage, so we need to find appropriate medicines. We can easily feel alone, isolated, so it helps greatly to make connection with other people. Important decisions await our attention, so we need to muster the courage to choose.

Moreover, at the top of any trouble, as at the bottom and around the sides, we find an inescapable mysteriousness. Why should it be that human beings can become alcoholics, or drug addicts, or people who cannot handle money, or people who abuse their spouses and children? Why should it be that disease can sweep in like a horrible wind and pass out a death sentence? Most people shy away from questions such as these, but then most people never get on top of their troubles. A good number endure, sometimes impressively so, but few appear to have passed through trouble into wisdom and peace. I want at least to help you believe there could come a day when you find a bit of wisdom, a patch of peace.

PEACE

I was about ten years old, walking home from school, trying to calm the panic rising from the fact that my father had resumed drinking, when suddenly

I stopped in the middle of the street. For the first time it struck me that I could do something about my panic. For the first time, I had a child's handle on trouble. I could think. I could put my mind to the matter of my panic. I could tell myself that even if my father had resumed drinking, it was not the end of the world. We had survived this before. Probably we would survive it again. The shame and the loss of money and all the rest need not defeat us. What the neighbors thought did not finally matter. What mattered was what God thought, and who could know what that was? What mattered was what I thought, and I knew I loved my father, despite my anger at him. He did not drink because he wanted to. He drank because he couldn't help himself.

I know it sounds strange to credit a ten-year-old with thoughts such as these, but trouble tends to make kids grow up quickly. To get some peace of mind, even kids may push and pull at their problems until lo, a new light dawns. The data rearrange themselves, and a calm breath of spirit enters the soul. Life is bigger than alcoholism, or cancer, or even bloody war. The wildflowers alongside the road hint at more: Life is beautiful as well as savage. The blue sky and sudden quiet of the birds promise that the future will have some good days, as well as more days filled with pain.

No one knows for sure where blessed moments

of peace like this come from. No one can tell me for sure why I cracked my problem that particular day and passed from being a child to being an adult. What anyone can say, though—anyone who studies how people cope with their problems—is that now and then things come together, at least momentarily, and we get a respite from our pain. For a little while our minds stop whirling and our bodies rest. Instinctively, we linger with the tranquillity and order visiting us. Without any reasoning we know that it is good for us to be in this place, this novel zone of our selves, where suffering does not touch us. Even though it usually moves off before long, such an experience of peace can sustain us for days to come. Thus in our reflections on techniques for handling trouble, we shall place much emphasis on ways of thinking, letting go of anxieties, sinking down to the bottom of our selves, that often move us toward peace.

DOING, THINKING, AND BEING

Even when I was a child, I realized that a problem like my father's drinking called for several different responses. There were things my mother, sister, and I could do, like finding his car outside a bar and going in to get him to come home; like trying to persuade him to try AA again. There were ways I could think, like preparing myself for the chance that he would not show up when he was supposed to pick me up and so arranging another way to get home. And though I would not have known how to put this when I was a child, there were also ways I could choose to be. I could be nervous and worried, or I could try to distance myself and keep my peace. When I prayed to God, I could ask for specific helps, but I could also say, "Your will be done." As a child I did not know how to separate different ways of thinking or praying so as to alter my being. But I did know, because it had hit me like a bolt of lightning in the street, that I could do many things about my troubles, if only I remembered to step back and think.

What a marvelous capacity this is, the human ability to step back and think. As far as we can tell, no other animal has it. The difference between our species and even the most intelligent nonhuman species is that we can reflect. At the same time, we can be both the defendant and the judge, both the object-to-be-studied and the subject-who-studies. I can take a look at my ideas and eventually improve them. I can remember my feelings, whether of joy or shame, and so learn what yesterday, or last week, or even twenty years ago still has to teach me. I can imagine again the conversation between the doctor and me when he told me I had bone cancer. I can project ahead, to the day when he may tell me that the only option left, other than surrendering to death, is a harrowing bone-marrow transplant. All this I can do, because I can "think." More than anything else in the human arsenal, thinking is our great weapon against trouble. When we have learned how to think our way to a peaceful being, as well as a practical doing, we have become mature human beings.

Many liberal-arts colleges advertise that they teach students to think. Usually the advertising is only a half truth. Usually our colleges teach people how to reason logically, how to read texts or analyze equations carefully, and perhaps how to line up pros and cons so as to make good decisions. Rarely do they teach people how to sift their feelings, or get to the center of their prejudices, or abandon themselves to the mysteriousness of life and so find an unearthly peace. In a word, our schools are at best only semicontemplative. They would blush to be caught speaking of contemplative prayer as the completion of any truly liberating education. They are much more at home with thinking than doing, and being leaves them quite puzzled. Yet they are among the few institutions in contemporary American culture that even come close to dealing with deep, ungimmicky techniques for handling trouble.

Look at American business, politics, law, or medicine, and you will find virtually nothing of spiritual substance. Look at popular American art, music, literature, or religion, and you will find a very mixed bag. Scripture says, "Without contemplation the people perish" (Prov. 11:14). One good way to characterize popular American culture is to say that our people are perishing for want of spiritual nourishment.

PHYSICAL PAIN

Want of spiritual nourishment is painful, and much realer than most cultural commentators recognize. But physical pain—withdrawal from alcohol or drugs, bones broken by myeloma, flesh beaten by abusive parents—defines a great many more dramatic troubles. The children of Ethiopia, Somalia, and other parts of drought-stricken, war-torn East Africa die painfully, witnesses to an enormous swath of trouble. The people with AIDS suffering horrible deaths trouble us, accuse us, in their every struggle. Homeless people walk the streets of a land of plenty. Who will shelter them from the cold or provide a warm meal? Their physical pains push them toward hopelessness, so every practical aid to their problem, every successful community response, is a victory for their spirits as well as their bodies. Physical pain alone ought to make our government reform the economy. The homeless and the victims of violence alone argue that we need a new social order.

People brought into trouble can realize how many others are also suffering. Yes, pain can make people turn narrow, become self-absorbed, but it can also make them realize that all over the world millions of others are suffering with them. When the sufferings seem to stem from stupid human policies, people brought into trouble have to fight a great temptation toward cynicism. When acts of God—natural disaster, lethal disease—are the cause, the problem is how not to curse the order of creation itself.

The Book of Job represents a classical treatment of this problem. Job suffers physically and spiritually, but he keeps trying not to curse God. Eventually, out of the whirlwind, God tells him that the problem of evil is too great for him. He did not make the world, so he cannot know its proportions. This is not completely satisfactory, but Job has to make do with it.

I can understand how physical pain can tempt people to call life a bad gift and wish they had never been born. I can say that until intense physical pain is neutralized, no one should be asked to think straight. But I still believe that pain need not be the whole story, even for those suffering it. I still believe that the human being is more than the body, just as a human life is more than food and clothing. When people in trouble are reminded of this more, they often regain much perspective.

REALISM

Reinhold Niebuhr, the leading American Protestant theologian of the 1940s and 1950s, once wrote on the back of an envelope a simple prayer. Taken up by Alcoholics Anonymous, it has become famous: "God, grant me serenity to accept the things I cannot change, courage to change the things I can, and wisdom to know the difference." In dealing with any trouble, we may hope eventually to learn this difference and so be realistic. Being realistic, we will not berate ourselves when we are unable to change things outside our control.

This wisdom comes especially hard when our troubles are caused by other people. If the alcoholism in question is that of a spouse or parent or child, we have limited control over it. If the disease in question comes out of the blue, as the legacy of bad genes or bad luck, we must at some point accept it as fated for us. In neither case does realism mean we should not try to prevent the spread of the trouble. We can work on the alcoholic spouse or parent. We can follow the regime of diet and exercise the doctor prescribes.

But much of the task of gaining peace of soul will boil down to accepting what we cannot change. To do this, most likely we shall have to think more deeply about life, fate, good luck and bad, than do our more fortunate neighbors.

That, of course, is not all bad—far from it. Shakespeare tells us that knowledge makes a "bloody entrance." The classical Greek dramatists constantly taught that wisdom comes through suffering. The price of becoming wise, or realistic to the point that we can help others, is usually having gone through much pain. The wisdom of people who have not suffered is suspect. Who can know how they will hold up when their own time of testing comes? Aristotle thought that no one should presume to teach ethics—what constitutes the good, fully human life —until after age fifty. Until fifty one simply does not have enough experience of suffering to teach others what is truly good and what is only apparently good.

The realism forced on us by significant trouble need not be grim, but it is bound to be serious. Only fools think they can get by on money and charm, laughter and gaiety. The world is a terrible place, as a visit to any third-world country shows. Certainly, third-world peoples can teach us much about loving life, celebrating life—but their poverty and deprivation make such teaching especially poignant. Not to be touched by such poignancy, to deal with the terrible sufferings of the world only at an emotional arm's length, is not to be "realistic" in any way I want to encourage. Dealing with trouble adequately forces us to enlarge our hearts.

How do we keep going, if we let ourselves feel the immense suffering of the poor? Indeed, how do we keep going if we simply walk through a cancer ward with eyes and ears open? Only by confronting the spiritual challenge in evil and suffering. As long as we keep running away, we remain unrealistic, immature, and vulnerable to being overwhelmed when trouble gets its claws into us. If our own ox is gored, and we have never faced the horrors possible in any life, we are likely to face despair.

DESPAIR

Despair means that we have lost hope. As long as the future stands open and we can hope to draw some good out of the evil we see or suffer, we need not despair. On analysis, then, it turns out that most despair arises because our focus has become too narrow. We have looked only at our own resources, found them woefully lacking, and so concluded that the future is hopeless. When we cast our net more broadly, availing ourselves of the resources of other people and the mysteriousness of life (the resources of God), our spirit may lighten. Other people may have good ideas about where we can gain some help. The mysteriousness of life may suggest that nothing is impossible with God, because God can make all things new. The mere possibility that this could be so is enough to drive away despair. To have realistic hopes, we need only recognize the possibility that we can outwit the cancer, at least for a while, or that AA might help our sick spouse, because it has helped so many other alcoholics.

Few things are more important for mental health, more precious, than hope. Whatever images stir hope in our hearts are healthy and good. Conversely, whatever images cast us down into despair are the enemy. We do not have complete control over the images that pass through our minds, but certainly we have some control. So "positive thinking," when it is not sappy, is a great ally in handling trouble. Later, when we deal more systematically with thinking and feeling, we shall pay close attention to the rise of images in imagination and the freedom that human intelligence has in determining how to use them. Seldom are we forced to accept images tempting us to despair. Almost always we can fight them off, because in fact we can never be sure about tomorrow—the future is always uncertain. Yes, this can cause some people great anxiety, but it can also free up the hope of others. If we are not looking for an unrealistic kind of security, we can find in the openness of the future a great stimulus to hope.

Despair also demonstrates that getting in shape to handle serious troubles requires us to remove ourselves, our egos, from the center of the stage. As long as we focus on our own limited resources, or even our own collection of hurts and pains, we are blind to many larger issues. Realism is much the same as healthy perspective. If we make ourselves the center of the universe, our perspective is not healthy, because clearly we are only a tiny speck poised in the midst of gigantic stretches of space and time. If we forget that we share the planet with well over five billion other human beings, we can think that all of nature and history have conspired against us, whereas the truth is that nature and history have paid us very little attention.

The Buddhists are wise about matters such as these. Since the time of the Buddha himself, they have seen that escaping from suffering and despair entails losing self-concern. When we get a proper perspective on our own smallness, a great many troubles fall away. It was never altogether pressing that we become great financial successes, or even that we live the normal span of seventy years. It was always possible that our role in the drama of nature and history was meant to be quite modest and so there was nothing we needed get overwrought about, let alone anything important enough to occasion despair.

JOY

Hope, like peace, is a sign that we are managing our troubles fairly well. Joy is a sign that we are managing our troubles very well. We cannot control joy. It is one of the graces that seems to move on the wind, coming and going as it chooses. That is the reason for the title of C. S. Lewis's famous book, *Surprised by Joy*. Nonetheless, people who have made their peace with their troubles, and have continued to hope that the mystery of life will give them a good future, tend to experience this surprise now and then. Sometimes the occasion is a beautiful day, when all seems right with the world. Other times the occasion is a small child, perfect in form and innocence. Falling in love can bring times of joy, especially early on, when it is clearest that genuine love is always a free gift. Creative work can leave us joyous, pleased beyond measure that the world can yield up great beauty and meaning.

Trouble seems to be the enemy of joy, and so it is for the most part. When we are troubled, it is hard to notice the beauty of the world, hard even to rejoice in the good fortune of our friends. But as we become accustomed to trouble, learning to live with an imperfect world and self, the conflict between trouble and joy can lessen. Indeed, we can grow to the point where we can find joy even in our pains, because we cannot separate them from the many good things in life. Trying as our alcoholic spouse may be, without him or her we would not have our children. Painful as our cancer may be, it can occasion from friends outpourings of love and support that take our breath away. So we should never turn our back on joy and think that trouble means joy will never visit again. If we keep faith with what our trouble wants to teach us, we may again hear the turtledove in the land.

Peace, hope, and joy are some of our most important guides through the dark forest of trouble. If we pay attention to what brings them into our spirit, we can learn precious things about our deepest spiritual needs. For example, we can realize that we must make peace with our trouble. Only when we have confronted it, taken its measure, and reconciled ourselves to its presence are we likely to be able to live without great anxiety. Similarly, we have to keep our hope of managing, even conquering, our trouble well stoked and glowing. Whatever tears down our hope, bringing us within sight of despair, is our enemy. Whatever builds up our hope is our friend. The same with joy, in contrast to deep sadness. Ultimately joy and deep sadness lie beyond our control, but if we think back to the sequence of images, feelings, and thoughts that usually accompany either one, sometimes we can find that early on we had a chance to deflect ourselves from sadness, or respond to overtures of joy. We had a chance to keep our spirits open to the divine mystery rather than close down and brood on our hurts. If we are to grow skillful in managing our troubles, we have to become alert to such chances. We cannot let them pass by unnoticed, unused, because we have no guarantee they will return again soon. We must seize the day, grab the opportunity—not like misers out to snatch at every penny, but like good students of time who realize that each day has its unique gifts and challenges.

THIS BOOK

I have suggested that this book offers old-fashioned techniques for handling trouble. Further, I have suggested that if we can get on top of our thinking, feeling, sharing with other people, making decisions, and praying, we will be in good shape. Inasmuch as I am proposing a close examination of these five activities, the method I am advocating boils down to familiarizing ourselves with an inventory of spiritual resources built into the human personality. When we have gained some understanding of how we think, feel, best share with others, make good decisions, and deal with the mysteriousness of our human situation, we are well equipped for handling trouble. When we do not have such an understanding, we are at the mercy of trouble, nearly certain to be run over.

My job will be to explain how I understand thinking, feeling, sharing with others, making decisions, and praying, in the light of their bearing on handling trouble. I shall have to make clear what each of these activities is and how it can help us clarify, accept, make real, shape, and finally pass beyond the trouble afflicting us. If my examples are apt enough, you should be able to identify in your own experience, your own trouble, the equivalent of what I am describing.

Your job will be to try to make such an identification, as well as to take to heart what I am saying about thinking, feeling, sharing, deciding, and praying. Initially, you may think that these activities are abstract, or that they make up an arbitrary list of human capacities. I urge you to make an act of faith that they are neither abstract nor arbitrary. In fact, they are the main things buzzing in each of our human interiors, and until we learn about them, we are unlikely to handle our troubles well.

Thus this is a book you should read slowly and critically. It is not offering you information so much as a map of your own spirit. The more you challenge what I say about thinking or feeling, sharing or deciding, the better will be your reading—the more help toward handling your troubles. Similarly, the better you come to understand what I am, and am not, saying about praying, the more help you will find for the deepest aspect of handling serious trouble—accepting what religious people call the will of God.

In asking you to read slowly and critically, I am hoping that you will savor the words I give you. Not because they will be brilliant or poetic, language the like of which you have never read before. Rather because, despite all their inadequacy, they come from and point toward the ultimate mysteriousness of life, which is an unfailing source of wonder and renewal. Words that lead us to this mystery are savory. They taste good, because they feed our souls.

We all know, in a tacit way, that life is greater than we are. We all seek a way to acknowledge this enormous, primitive fact without feeling overwhelmed. When we find words that lead us into the mystery and make it congenial—make it the place we were meant to abide—we tend to call those words precious. They have shown us ways to a better self, one more peaceful, hopeful, and joyous than the workaday version. Indeed, they have shown us why trouble can never be the first or last word about us— how we should be defined by wonder and love more than by ignorance and death.

After I have dealt with thinking, feeling, sharing, deciding, and praying, I shall summarize my convictions in the form of an outline of a practical method. It will not seem new, after you have been through Chapters Two through Six, but it may help you begin to attack your troubles systematically. With practice the method becomes habitual—a regular cast of mind. At that point, probably any new trouble will not be especially threatening, because you have grown confident that thinking about it, clarifying your feelings, working it over with friends, making what decisions you must, and praying so as to place it in ultimate perspective will cut it down to size.

CHAPTER ONE

Thinking

OVERVIEW

IN THIS CHAPTER WE BEGIN OUR INVENTORY OF how our minds work and how we may best use them to ease our troubles. Nine subtopics engage our attention.

First, we consider *data*—facts, information, what we need to know to get our bearings. Most troubles imply enormous amounts of information, only a little of which is directly relevant to muddling through. For example, to understand the basic processes of multiple myeloma takes only about fifteen minutes. However, to get on top of all the current research would require specialized training in biochemistry that lies beyond most of us. Similarly, to understand the basic facts of a given case of alcoholism is seldom difficult: Peter gets depressed at his job prospects and staggers home drunk; Jill feels unattractive and so hides in the bottle. However, to cure Peter or Jill may well be a long, painful enterprise. One may have to learn reams about them and show the patience of Job. On the way to that, it is boon enough for those who have to live with Peter or Jill to work out strategies for helping them get work or feel more attractive, as well as strategies for coping with the drunks they go on when their hopes crash.

Second, related to data are techniques for gathering *information*. Many people stay stuck in first gear, unable to make much progress with their troubles, because they do not possess crucial information, are unaware of helps available to them. Thus, it is worth sketching how to go about gathering information—how to become a small-scale, part-time researcher. Once you learn that the telephone directory, or the local research librarian, is a marvelous source of information, the task of gathering helpful information starts to look easy rather than impossible.

Third, we deal with *imagining*. Most of what we can do depends on what we can imagine. As we shall discover when dealing with feelings, images have a great power to dominate our emotions. In this chapter, however, we are concerned more with the role that images play in understanding. Until we get apt images, we are not likely to crack our problems, to see the light. Thus it helps to discuss how the human imagination tends to work and suggest ways of harnessing it to the task at hand.

Fourth, we deal with *understanding* proper. When we understand we say, "Aha." A light dawns. The data fall into a pattern that makes sense. We see our way to some practical consequences—some concrete ways of attacking our problem. And, as a result of any of these good things, we feel encouraged. We're no longer in the dark. We've started to make progress toward the light, the day when we feel in control. Understanding is always in part a function of our native intelligence. The education we have received to date is also a factor. But typically people underestimate their ability to grasp what is happening to them. In fact, real trouble can bring out an intelligence, geared to survival, that makes us equal to the tasks our trouble sets us. Thus, understanding our understanding tends to be encouraging. We realize we are made to get the point. If people will be patient with us, and we will be patient with ourselves, we can master much more than we initially expect.

Fifth, we deal with *judging,* which differs somewhat from understanding. Understanding produces bright ideas, things that may be so, hypotheses. Judging is the process of checking out our bright ideas, finding whether they hold water. It *may* be a good idea to put fifty thousand dollars into your cousin's new bologna business, but it may also be the way to lose your shirt. If you are prudent, you will ask many questions about the business he is starting and not give him your money until you're convinced he's prepared a good thing. Wise people are those with good judgment. Wise people have a nose for what is bologna and what is prime rib. They do not act on every bright idea. They take time for testing, getting more information, assuring themselves an idea is solid.

Sixth, one of the key moments in a good process of judging comes when we take stock of our *prejudgments*—the prejudices, in favor or against, that we brought to the matter in question. Suppose, for example, that you never could stand luncheon meat. Or suppose, to the contrary, that you've loved bologna, ballpark franks, salami and pepperoni and Polish sausage since the cradle. To make a good decision about your cousin's venture, you'd better get your feelings about bologna out on the table. Otherwise, irrational factors could cloud your judgment. Otherwise, pictures of luscious sandwiches could leave you fifty thousand dollars poorer.

Seventh, having gone through some of the operations that constitute thinking, I invite you to take possession of your mind and learn how to *enjoy* it.

Thinking should be a pleasure. Learning should be lifelong and delightful. However, so many people have bad memories of school that perhaps a majority of the population limps along without such pleasure and delight. That is a shame, because it inhibits careful, disciplined thinking and so keeps millions mired in their troubles more than they need be.

When we do not feel pressured, as though the worst of our old teachers were popping a quiz, our minds are naturally inquisitive. Indeed, they are even naturally judicious: When calm, we are quick to sniff out nonsense, slow to get taken in by wild ideas. And this judiciousness, like solving practical puzzles, brings with it a distinctive pleasure. For then we know that we are being especially human, are exercising uniquely human gifts.

Eighth, I say a few things about *intellectual patience,* which is a virtue especially useful to people who find themselves in trouble. The more we can quiet our minds and pay attention, the more likely we are to get a handle on our troubles—start to bring them under our control. The first step to bringing them under our control is understanding the mess we find ourselves in: how we got there, what the proportions of our trouble are. In the beginning our great enemy is panic. Intellectual patience defends us against panic, both in the beginning and through to the end.

Ninth and last, we deal with intellectual *peace*. This tends to occur at the end of struggling with our troubles, but we can also experience it while in the middle. The major stimulus to a sense of intellectual peace is a little progress in understanding where we find ourselves. As soon as we make progress, we start to think that the situation is not hopeless. Then it becomes possible to relax a bit, gather our confidence, and enjoy a patch of peace. We may experience deep peace only when our trouble is resolved completely. Only a full remission of cancer or Jill's having gone five years without a drink may let us feel completely free of anxieties. But every bit of progress in understanding our situation and mastering it invites us to trust that we can do the job handed us. And every increase in such trust invites us to be peaceful—confident that the divine mystery holds us in good hands.

DATA

We begin with data. Data are facts, "givens," the information determining the trouble or situation in which we find ourselves. We are so many years old, so many dollars wealthy, in such and such health, possessed of such and such a history. This is the first, or the fifth, or the eleventh time that we've bounced a check, mismanaged our finances, gotten ourselves in an embarrassing corner. Last time we swore off credit cards. Why did we get a new Visa and start overspending again? Last time we went to a credit counselor. Why did we lurch off the budget on which she placed us?

These are the kinds of facts and questions we need to assemble at the outset of dealing with any given trouble. Often we know all the relevant facts, at least the first tier, because they are part of our life's story. But sometimes we do not know them, especially when our trouble comes from someone else, and often there are further facts we ought to consider, though we don't realize this at the outset.

In general, we cannot have too much information about our situation. Yes, a few people tend to overdose on facts, usually as a protection against making decisions. But many more people remain stuck in their troubles because they are too stunned or afraid to start investigating—assembling the basic facts. Like a good reporter, we need to know, minimally, who-what-where-when-how-why. Who is this guy that cannot stop taking dope? What does his dope problem amount to in terms of money spent, time wasted, jobs lost, people hurt, damage to his health, and so forth? Where does he get his dope, take it, hang out with fellow addicts? When did he begin, when does he usually shoot up, when has he ever stopped or shown remorse? How does he talk about his problem, think about it? How might you stop his current patterns of drug abuse, protect yourself from the harm they are doing you, safeguard your children from following him? Why do you find yourself in this situation? Why didn't you see he was becoming addicted? Why did you marry him in the first place?

Some readers of this book will find that the data most relevant to their situation show them locked into behavior that is obsessive or compulsive. They keep overspending, or overeating, or drinking too much. Habitually they use tranquilizers wrongly, or beat their kids, or engage in incest. The first step toward changing this behavior is acknowledging it. Perhaps nothing is more courageous, more to be encouraged. When the data accuse us of serious wrongdoing, we have to treasure reform—the restoration of what is right—more than any image of righteousness. Any people who help us believe that honoring what is right is worth the great pain it can require are great benefactors. Anytime we realize the challenge latent in "facing the facts," we sense the claims of God on our conscience. It can sound fashionable, glib, to call people of conscience "heroes." The plain reality, though, is that telling the truth, owning up to the facts about one's life and self, is the foundation of all maturity. There are no heroes in God's sight who are not people of conscience. There are no saints, no admirable pilgrims even, who fudge the facts and refuse to begin at the beginning.

Some of the questions at the beginning are clearly painful. Even the first step toward thinking clearly about your trouble—gathering what basic information you can—may make high demands. So you've got to realize, perhaps by getting others to reinforce the fact, that until you take your head out of the sand and face up to the facts, you'll never make any progress. Your pain will only continue, in all probability getting worse. Your frustration and fear will keep mounting, because you'll be like an animal, scampering around without understanding.

In the beginning of any cure, any good handling of trouble, lies a great act of courage: facing the facts. When you are able to say, "I have cancer and must do something about it," or "I am an alcoholic; clearly I need help," or "Jay shows all the signs of being a cokehead; I've got to find out," you're on the way to changing your bad situation.

GETTING INFORMATION

American culture is big on information. With only a little effort, it is possible to find out all sorts of things. When they learned I had cancer of the bone marrow, several of my industrious friends swung into action. One went to the medical library at the Stan-

ford Medical School and photocopied a dozen ab-
stracts of articles about multiple myeloma. Another
sent me protocols for bone-marrow transplants that
had come before a national medical committee on
which he had been serving. When I combined this
information with what my doctors had told me, I
felt I knew more than enough to understand what
was happening to me and why I was getting the
treatment my oncologist prescribed.

Had I been on my own, it might have taken me
a little longer to amass such information, but the task
would not have been difficult. I would have gone to
the library, consulted volumes dealing with cancer,
checked out books, and copied articles. I would have
called the hotline of the American Cancer Society
and/or dropped by their local office for advice and
pamphlets. (I did this at the local office of the Arthritis Foundation, when the initial diagnosis of my
back trouble was arthritis.)

I have been trained to use libraries, and I've
learned that the judicious use of the yellow pages
often can move me from total ignorance to adequate
knowledge in as little as a morning. However, many
people in our society are not so familiar with techniques for gathering information. They know that
we live in a computerized world, but they need help
to get access to information that is relevant to their
trouble. Let them rest assured that nine times out of
ten librarians and technicians will be more than glad

to help them. That is a librarian's job and great satisfaction.

Often the information people need is practical, so the best place to start can be with social-welfare agencies. If the problem is drugs, alcohol, delinquent children, delinquent payments of child support, the best place to learn about legal rights or available programs is likely to be a social-welfare office of the city, or the county, or a local church district. The first office you choose may not be the most pertinent, but usually people in that office will tell you what other office is better.

Let us call people who have specialized information "experts" and reflect for a moment on the role they play. An expert possesses technical information that laypeople do not. Some experts are available at no cost, or low cost, through social-welfare agencies. Others charge dearly for their time, but an hour of it can prove a godsend. For example, if you need to know your legal rights in acquiring a divorce, then access to an attorney is imperative. A good attorney can tell you in an hour what it could take you a week to find out on your own (assuming that you could unravel the technical terminology). The same with a good accountant. If your trouble involves taxes and money management, it may be well worth your while to spend what a good accountant would charge to go over your financial affairs and give you advice.

Many people increase their troubles because they will not or cannot consult experts and so rely on the advice of friends who really do not know. In medical matters, legal matters, and financial matters, this can be disastrous. In emotional matters each case is unique, but unless your lay friends are stable and wise, they may be bad sources of advice about how to bring your emotions to even keel. One litmus test is how well ordered, how happy and peaceful, their own lives are.

Thus, when we think of gathering the information necessary to illuminate our problems and show us the relevant options, we should think in terms of both researching on our own and consulting experts. Sometimes we can gather most of what we need ourselves, by acquiring access to banks of relevant data. Other times we will need the advice of specialists, people who work every day on cancer or taxes or depression. The crucial thing is to take enough initiative to track down the right sources. Usually, if we keep asking pertinent questions, keep following up leads and not letting ourselves become discouraged, in a surprisingly short time we will find the book or expert we need. This will not necessarily solve our problem completely, because evaluations and decisions may remain that only we can make; but it will constitute enormous progress, and it will encourage us considerably.

IMAGINING

Suppose your problem is budgeting. You never have any money left at the end of the month. Again and again you find you have postponed saving. What is your image, the picture in your mind, of how you handle money? How does it square with what you actually do? Have you ever kept track of where your money goes day by day? Have you ever forced yourself to account for every penny? If you imagined yourself as a vigorous army commander, come to take control of a troubled battle area, perhaps you would be willing to watch your spending closely. If you pictured dramatically the consequences of your not saving regularly—for example, imagining your children disappointed at not being able to go to college—you might be willing to change your ways.

When I got out of the hospital and started to rehabilitate my back and leg, I recalled old images of how I used to exercise before I took sick. At one time I was a demon swimmer, going back and forth for as many as 150 laps of the twenty-five-yard pool at our apartment complex (over two miles). As soon as I could manage, I hobbled down to the pool with my walker. At first I was completely discouraged: I could not swim more than four strokes. My leg went right to the bottom, heavy and terribly sore. Nonetheless, I kept thinking about the old days, when swimming was a joy—as easy and effortless as walking. A week later I managed to make it across the pool. The next day I managed to swim a lap lengthwise. Within six weeks I was up to half a mile.

Certainly, I could not have done this if I had not been recuperating physically—if my body had not been healing, my blood had not been bouncing back. But I also could not have done it if I had not imagined my way beyond my initial incapacity. I kept thinking of how easy swimming is when one knows how to do it, when one is completely relaxed and confident. I kept trying to remember how good I used to feel after vigorous exercise, and how once I had gotten into shape, I would feel I could go on forever. I bolstered my hopes of renewing my swimming by listening again to the voice of my doctor as he encouraged me with great enthusiasm. I made myself linger with the images that came when I found I could walk in the water unaided, long before I could take an independent step on dry land.

In a word, I made my imagination my ally—not because I was a genius, but because I knew, from studying the imagination, how important positive images are. Deliberately, I pictured myself as Mark Spitz, Matt Biondi, all the other great Olympic swimmers I had ever watched. I might only be able to go at a fraction of their speed, and my right leg might kick awkwardly, but still I was one of their peers, another water bug filling his lungs and helping his bones by stroking forward lap after lap. Of course, all the pretty girls cheered, and I was not loath to take a bow.

It was funny, and it was tragic, this number I did on myself, but it got the job done. Now I'm walking without a cane, and soon I'll be swimming a mile a day (having gone up by increments of two laps a week). The limits of our performances are often the limits of our imaginative ingenuity. So take a look at how you are using your imagination. Challenge yourself to become more creative—to picture new ways to handle your trouble. Be tough with yourself, gentle with yourself, whatever you find encouraging. Give your daydreams some direction, and fight your nightmares so they leave you alone. You can do this. You have some say about what lives in your head. The better guests you establish, the more likely you are to think effectively and work well.

UNDERSTANDING

As I noted in the overview, the act of understanding proper is an insight, the flash of light in which we say, "Aha!" Perhaps the easiest way for me to illustrate it is to ask you to solve the following problem. Consider this sequence of numbers, then place in the blank slot at the end the number that ought to follow: 2 8 4 1 5 20 16 4 ___. (Use the following blank space as a work sheet.)

The only way you can complete the sequence confidently, knowing that your entry is correct and not just a guess, is to have cracked the code that relates the numbers. If they are really a sequence as you've been told, and not just a random listing, they are related by a formula. A formula expresses a reason, a pattern, a set of intelligible connections. Understanding is precisely the grasp of a reason, a pattern, a set of intelligible connections among the data we are pondering. It is precisely grasping how the data "fit together," how they "make sense."

The number that should go in the blank at the end of the sequence is 8. Apart from a wild guess, the only way you can know this is by having understood that the formula connecting the numbers is $\times 4 - 4 \div 4 + 4$. After 8 the sequence would repeat, yielding 32 28 7 11. If you have the formula, you can keep playing the sequence out endlessly.

I hope that you did crack the code, and not merely look ahead for the answer, because if you did, you experienced an insight. You began in puzzlement, seeing only randomness. Apart from intuition, which a few people have for numbers, the only way you could have passed from randomness to understanding was to examine the relationship between given numbers. So you would have asked yourself how 2 relates to 8, and the most obvious answers would have been +6 and ×4. Then you would have asked yourself how 8 relates to 4. Again, several relations would have been obvious: ÷2 and −4. The relation of 4 to 1 would have called forth ÷4 and −3. The relation of 1 to 5 would have called forth +4 and ×5.

At this point, if you were astute, you would have noticed all the variations, the permutations, of 4. Moving to the relation between 5 and 20, you would have considered ×4 more promising than +15, all the more so since you would have seen that ×4 repeated the first relation in the series (between 2 and 8). When you verified that the relation of 20 to 16 repeated the second relation in the series, −4, you would have sniffed victory. The relation between 16 and 4 (÷4) would have confirmed your confidence that you had cracked the code, so you would have entered (+4) 8 in the last box with a flourish.

The insight proper was the point when you said, "Aha! It's the four different things one can do with 4: multiply, subtract, divide, and add." You might have only stitched this together in pieces, but at some point a little light would have dawned. With its dawning would have come a telltale pleasure. However silly or insignificant the puzzle, you would have been proud to have solved it. Hang on to this pleasure. It is very human. In the midst of agonizing efforts to understand a serious problem, a heavy-weight trouble, every little bit of enlightenment is precious.

Why? Because every little bit of enlightenment, insight, tells us we are right to work hard at solving our troubles—that the demanding, sometimes boring business of thinking through the relations between problematic terms is worthwhile. We have been created to understand—it is our birthright as human beings. Even when we cannot understand fully (as, for example, when we come up against such mysteries as genetic inheritance or bad free choices), we can sense that we were right to push forward to these barriers. Indeed, if we learn that Peter's mother was also an alcoholic, and her father before her, we can take some consolation. If we find out that Lisa treated her first husband much the same as she's treating her second, we can say that her irresponsible or cruel behavior is characteristic. This does not tell us how to change her behavior, but it does tell us we were not crazy to think her strange or abnormal. It does bring our problem with her—our trouble—into sharper focus, and so advance the day when we can come to terms with it successfully.

JUDGING

Judging follows on understanding. After we have gained an insight, we ought to ask, "Is this so? Have I grasped the point accurately?" With a number sequence we might ask for further digits, to make sure that the formula we came up with does in fact fit. In the laboratory, scientists keep testing their hypotheses, making sure that their formulas solve or predict all the relevant ranges of data. The practiced academic interviewer may ask to see some of the books that the candidate claims to have written, or may at least look them up in Books in Print. The practiced child of an alcoholic parent will check speech, gait, facial appearance, and mental sharpness before accepting the parent's claim not to have been drinking, merely to be tired. I could tell from the sound of my father's foot on the stair whether or not he had been drinking. Ten years old, I knew whether he was drunk or sober as soon as I'd heard two sentences over the phone. And by then I knew that my own judgment, not what he told me, was the reality to depend on, because again and again my suspicions had proved correct while his protestations had proved to be lies.

In handling troubles, we are always in need of good judgment. We have to assess the data we have gathered. We have to determine the reliability of the advice, even the expert advice, we have received. Sometimes this is quite easy. For example, if doctors dealing with cancer each day (oncologists) have set up standard procedures for chemotherapy, the odds are probably in favor of the judgment that it is best to submit our cancer to such procedures, unless one has solid evidence that medical practice in general is corrupt.

On the other hand, if you are dealing with highly experimental procedures, the caution lights should go on. Lacking a lot of information, even an adequate amount of experience with such procedures, the doctors in charge ought to be quite tentative. If you find them giving you assurances or even hopes that go far beyond what any test results can support, you ought to become suspicious of their medical judgment, and so of their usefulness to you. The same, analogously, with lawyers or accountants or theologians whom you find going beyond the data, offering you assurances that you realize, on reflection, they cannot back up. For instance, every good theologian will tell you that God loves you, and so there can be a silver lining in any trouble. No good theologian will tell you exactly what that silver lining will be—exactly how God's love is bound to work out. Only an idolater, one who thinks he or she knows the mind of God fully, will attempt to tell you that.

Parallel to the delight, the natural pleasure, that insight brings is the satisfaction that working in your spiritual depths to make good judgments can bring. If you linger leisurely with the pulls and counterpulls involved in coming to a serious judgment, you will find that you like feeling weighty, being forced to sharpen your intuitions, to check out lines of reasoning, to go back over what the data actually say, and to stir up your confidence that you can finally separate what is likely to be so from what is unlikely to be so—what is not to be accepted uncritically.

Certainly, making serious judgments is painful, trying, at times even wrenching. But we are constructed to do this. The calm that good judgment requires, the detachment and dedication needed to determine what actually is so, rather than what we might like to be so or what everyone says is so, are mature spiritual qualities. We should not become stodgy or self-satisfied if we find we have developed these qualities, but we should enjoy getting down to basics and asserting our responsibility to judge for ourselves whether what we have been told is actually false or true.

CRITICIZING PREJUDGMENTS

A crucial moment in judgment is the time when we check our prejudices. Perhaps nothing else teaches us more about ourselves. For example, even as a child I had to deal with the question of whether I *wanted* my father to be drunk. In the beginning almost everything in me did not, so I bent over backward to accept his protestations of sobriety. But

after he had let me down again and again, I found
that a growing part of me wanted to be able to write
him off. If I could be sure that he was sure to be
drunk, I could put him in a box labeled "bad actor"
and not suffer any complexity. But on occasion, in
fact, he was not drunk. And as he grew older, he did
better with AA, sometimes going for the better part
of a year without drinking. So even as a teenager I
realized that honesty required my keeping an open
mind. If he was more than fifteen minutes late for
dinner, I still suspected that he had begun drinking
again, but I had to refrain from making that judgment until I saw him with my own eyes.

We are complicated creatures, and never more
so than when we are in pain. If someone has hurt us
consistently, we can begin to protect ourselves by
simplifying that person's reality and significance—by
telling ourselves that he or she can only be a source
of pain. Yet few people are so simple. Even if they
hurt us eight or nine times out of ten, every once in
a while they do something nice—all the more so if
they love us, or once protested that they did. So most
of the involved interpersonal pains that beset us
make us face up to complicated feelings and prejudices. It hurts to consider how our love has been
wasted, what fools we have been, but we have to
keep such hurt from making us write off completely
those who disappoint us. If we want to be fair (as our
conscience requires us to be) we have to leave the

door open a little. When the person who disappoints us does something good, we have to be able to register it.

Perhaps even more difficult are the prejudgments we make about ourselves. The more pain we are in—because of failures of judgment, botched loves, thwarted goals—the more we can come to expect to fail. Down on ourselves, we can give ourselves no chance of succeeding. Without confidence we can read every difficulty as a sign that we are bound to screw things up again. And so, fulfilling this prophecy, we can make mistake after disastrous mistake. One sees this happen between parents and children. A father can become sure that he will never be able to handle his rage at his children's insubordination and so cut them off emotionally rather than deal with the pain they give him, the failure they make him feel. A wife can become sure she will always fail her husband's expectations or hopes, will never be as pretty or bright as he wants. Then, bitterly and sadly, she can write their marriage off, setting her face for endurance and concluding that she is a failure.

Anyone privy to people's inmost thoughts and feelings, especially those that express how they regard themselves, knows that few human beings think too well of themselves. Apart from a few buffoons, most women and men think themselves unlovable.

They do not believe that their lovers or friends would love them if they knew them to the depths of their souls. They do not believe that God can love them, despite all the religious talk about God's love having no preconditions. So they can never be naked, psychologically. They can never feel fully honest, not a fraud. Thus they tend to limp along, even when successful at work and apparently enjoying a fine family life. The full joy and peace for which they have been made, for which they long, never quite possess them. The quiet desperation of which poets speak erodes their satisfaction. Until they are able to confront the harshness with which they judge themselves, they are not likely to be fully happy.

ENJOYING THINKING

If you have taken pleasure in the reflections in this chapter, you enjoy thinking about thinking. A part of you feels drawn to the interior life. You are fascinated by your spiritual processes, and you sense that the more you understand them, the better off you are likely to be. On the other hand, if you have found the sections of this chapter hard going, you probably find interior realities foreign, unfamiliar, and frightening. If you have persevered, nonetheless, you have a strong character—or a large need.

We ought to enjoy thinking, reflecting, imagining—all the main activities of the spiritual life. We ought to enjoy inner quiet, simply waiting on the divine mystery. To balance our active engagement with nature and our fellow human beings, we need a private, personal life in which we can "center down," as the Quakers like to say. In early morning, or during a noontime break, or in the evening after the kids have gone to bed, we ought to let our desires, our preoccupations, even our worries, fade away, and for a little while just *be*—just stay quiet and listen to our deeper ebb and flow.

Classical Chinese culture tried to blend Confucianism and Taoism. Confucianism was a system of manners derived from Master K'ung, who was roughly a contemporary of the Buddha 2,500 years ago. Taoism was a theory of action based on how the "Way" (Tao) of nature moved. Its most influential text was the *Tao Te Ching* (The Way and Its Power), attributed to Lao-tzu, who probably lived a century after Master K'ung.

Ideally, cultured Chinese people lived according to the motto, "In office a Confucian, in retirement a Taoist." "Office" was the world of politics, business, secular affairs. "Retirement" was the world of the arts, philosophy, inward reflection. The Confucians codified social relations. They helped people know exactly what a "gentleman," a person of breeding, education, and refinement, would do in important situations. The Taoists were preoccupied with the "Way" of nature. They thought that by emptying one's mind of human conventions, one could gain harmony with a wilder, more creative legislation or pathway, the patterns of nature itself. Wisely, traditional China recognized that each outlook, each school, had its wisdom.

In this book we are more Taoist than Confucian, though of course any concern to be practical and help people navigate through the paper or bureaucracy standing between them and help makes us Confucian. Our main point, though, is that most voices of self-help neglect the resources of the traditional schools of contemplation. Most accept the extroversion of current American culture and pay little attention to people's ability to learn the needs, the structures, of their own spirits. A Taoist such as Lao-tzu tells us to "shut the doors" and go within. The doors are the senses. Within is the spirit, nourished by the senses but also frequently overloaded by them.

To enjoy thinking, we have to discipline the senses. After we have let them make their contribution (let them give us relevant data and images), we should concentrate on activating our inner resources —the reason, imagination, feeling, discernment, that can put such data and images together in fitting, creative combinations. The productive writer, for example, often relies more on fresh possibilities found in common data than on new information. Similarly, think of how many different ways artists or designers can recast primary colors, basic geometric patterns, the relations between shoulder and waist, between thigh and ankle. The same with the person trying to get a handle on a practical problem. Sometimes new information provides new leads, but many other times one succeeds by going more deeply into the implications of old, familiar information.

Above all, going more deeply in this fashion suggests meeting one's own mind, coming to terms with one's own needs, prejudices, assumptions, abilities both to hang in and to let go. Suppose, for instance, that I am hurt by my friend, who seems not to hear my cries of pain, my cries for attention. If I think about this reaction, asking whether my hurt is justified, I risk finding that I am overly needy, a bit of a baby. However, I also activate a pleasing self-criticism, a self-justifying move to live in the light. Yes, I may be especially needy right now, because I am afraid of the cancer within me. But no, I am not neurotic in asking for help. She promised her support, and I did not ask her to trek to Nepal. I only asked her to read a book. That she did not even register my request, that it never even lodged in her computer, was bound to hurt me. Love pays attention. Love notices things, because it is wholly interested in the beloved. Not to notice is not to love, to be a poor friend.

Even though it is painful to conclude that my friend's love is limited, it is good to get to the bottom of our relationship, get some clarity on what I can and cannot expect. I am made for such clarity, and so are you. We cannot obtain it once and for all. We have to go after it, find it anew, week after week. But it is what Christians call the Kingdom of God within us, the Holy Spirit at work.

Most of what we need to gain peace and happiness lies within. If we have food and clothing, shelter and a community, we can survive physically. Emotional survival, prospering by feeling that our lives are wonderful gifts, depends on our ability to appreciate the beauty of nature, the gratuity of friends, and the marvels of our own spirit. One such marvel is that constantly we can grow. Almost always we can learn, even from painful mistakes. Equally, almost always we can finally see that our lives are short, and the mystery of life, of nature, of God, is very long. So in a blessed sense we don't matter terribly much. We can let ourselves go, let that mystery take care of us. We all die, sooner or later. The great trick is to draw from this inevitability the ability to live, day after day, with a growing depth and freedom. You will never find this gift in isolation. Always it comes accompanied by an enjoyment of thinking, the contemplative life, getting to the depth of your human spirit, where the great questions of overall meaning lodge.

INTELLECTUAL PATIENCE

"Patience" suggests waiting quietly. It also suggests suffering. Both suggestions are important, if we would learn how to handle trouble well. We have to give ourselves time to figure out the mess in which we find ourselves. We also have to put up with feeling foolish, or threatened, or demeaned. The better we understand our minds and hearts, the more gracefully we can exercise this patience.

A cancer patient longs for a remission. That is the point to the chemotherapy or radiation. The goal is to beat the cancer back, ideally to eradicate it. The hope is that one can again live without malignancy. But achieving a remission is not the end of one's trial. Few remissions are guaranteed to the natural limit of one's years. Five years is a ballpark figure after which one can hope, with many kinds of cancer, that the malignancy is gone definitively. But the cloud never leaves the cancer patient's horizon. The possibility of recurrence always hangs around.

In addition, remission can bring a certain letdown. Anatole Broyard's good book, *Intoxicated by My Illness*, reveals a curious secret. A mortal illness sets you on full alert. Your adrenaline flows. You feel more alive because you must gather all your resources. The same with other challenges, other major troubles. Because crisis is intoxicating, energizing, people can become crisis junkies. After working in the emergency room, other kinds of medicine can seem tame. After managing the desk at the domestic-violence intervention center, ordinary counseling can be a drag.

Remission returns you to the ordinary mass of people. No longer are you so unique as once you were. Yes, you carry less stigma, less oddity, which is certainly a significant relief. But you also carry less drama. You also have less authority in matters of life and death. So you have to live along a strange border, in love with life but ready at a moment's notice to don again the T-shirt of the dying. You can be consoled to think that we all ought to live this way, as the medievals taught: *Memento mori* (remember death). But you've got to learn a new sort of patience. Your disease is the leader, you are the follower. If you are to dance gracefully, you've got to follow smoothly, willingly, giving up your will to another.

Religious people can be helped greatly at this juncture by making God the leader. The dance unfolds as God desires. In giving up their own will, they can hope to be taking on the will of God. People who are not religious are under the same necessity, but how to picture it, understand it, is less clear. Should they say they must take each day as fate passes it out to them? Can they fight harder to bend fate to their own will? Dylan Thomas is famous for urging us to rage, rage against dark death, and there's something winning in his urging. If we love life, we have to hate death—or do we?

Saint Francis of Assisi spoke of death as our sister. Many Eastern sages tell us to be indifferent, accepting death as completely natural, placing ourselves beyond any concern about either living or dying. They seem to have a good point. Death is spoken into our being, inscribed in our genetic codes. From the beginning the tiny infant is made to end in the grave. So death cannot be completely foreign to us. It must be that we can always find it in our bones. To deny that we are always mortal is to run from one of the most basic truths. Thus Ernest Becker and many others have criticized the way we refuse to think about death, the way we separate ourselves and our children from the dying, the fraud we perpetrate in our wakes and funerals.

At the bottom of our minds, where our thinking runs out, we find that we are bound to suffer. The last word about us, as the first word, does not come from our own mouths. A great mystery surrounds us, and we have no peace until we reconcile ourselves to it. We must suffer not knowing when we will end, how we will end, what our lives will finally have meant. This mystery does not remove the need for patience with trials such as divorce or the loss of a job. It does not take away their sting. But it does remind us that, as the Buddhists say in their "first noble truth," all life is suffering. To be in pain is nothing unusual. Indeed, to be human is to be forced to be patient, to move to a foreign music and will. The better we think our way to our bed-rock human condition, the more interesting and liberating our suffering can become.

INTELLECTUAL PEACE

The classical definition of "peace," attributed to Saint Augustine, is "the tranquillity of order." When we get our lives together, our spirits can lie at rest. The consideration of suffering and death that we passed through in the prior section was meant precisely to indicate what we must deal with if we are to get our lives together. The divorce or loss of a job or serious illness now giving us trouble is only part of our problem as human beings. Certainly, we can believe that it is the most pressing part and so think that ruminating about suffering and death is beside the point. In fact, however, this belief is shortsighted. In fact, our divorce or loss of a job or heart disease comes into perspective only when we understand that if one problem does not beset us, another soon will. At the least, one day some years from now we shall have to deal with old age, and then dying. There is no way to solve the problem of life once and for all. There is no way not to suffer and fear—unless we learn to accept our human condition.

The movement of our mind is on our side. As soon as we force ourselves to pay attention to our trouble, to stop running away in panic, we begin a process whose natural end is our peace. For as soon as we think about our ruined marriage, or our sorry job prospects, or the screwups of our children, we inevitably notice that this is not our first experience of suffering. Also, we remember that other people have gone through divorces, and the loss of jobs, and their children's screwups. Then, sighing, we can at least take comfort in the fact that our present trouble is not unusual.

We experienced failure as teenagers, if not before. We've known pain for more years than we like to count. And all our friends have told us stories of hardship, regret, loss. We haven't known anyone whose life has been untroubled. Bill, a wonderful guy, came home one day to find that his wife had declared herself a long-repressed lesbian and gone off with another woman. Joe, the best of teachers, suffered through two years of uncertainty about tenure only to lose his job because his publications weren't up to the mark his school set. Sam finally realized his dream of becoming a college president, but two years later he was out in the cold, fired because of conflicts with his board of trustees. Sally, apparently so warm and bouncy, has never recovered fully from the stillbirth of one of her twins. Hanna, the leader of our social circle, has had one breast removed and now learned that the lumps in the other must be biopsied.

A traditional African story sums up the lesson. A woman whose son had died went to a tribal elder complaining bitterly. He listened patiently and then said to her, "Take a trip. Travel the whole circuit of the surrounding villages. When you find a family that has never known suffering, come back to me, and we will arrange a trial to accuse God." Needless to say, the trial never happened. The woman could find no family untouched by pain of some sort. That did not return her son or remove her suffering. It did remove her illusion that God had singled her out for special malice.

When we deal with prayer in Chapter Five we shall consider the matter of why God allows suffering. We shall get no certain answer, but it will be good to grapple with the question. Here the point is that peace of mind requires an acceptance of suffering. After we have done our best to remove pain, escape suffering, we finally have to admit that no life has passed untroubled. Certainly, we should struggle against our troubles. Not to do so would be masochistic—a perverse endorsement of suffering. But our struggle must be realistic. No matter how dramatic the victories we manage, old age and death still await us. No matter how long our remission or how happy our second marriage, pain remains a certainty, sure as the turning of the seasons.

Qoheleth, the depressed voice of Old Testament wisdom, says that all life is vanity: "Vanity of vanities, and all is vanity." He says this kindly as well as sadly. For he hopes to keep us from the delusion of expecting a lasting happiness. Only if we set our hopes on something outside the turning world of human troubles (for him, the will of God) can we protect ourselves from heavy sorrow. As long as we think that money or pleasure, success or human accomplishment, will satisfy us uninterruptedly, we remain sorry fools. The follies of our children, or the decline of our health, or the change in political fortunes will upset us mightily. As the prophet Isaiah put it, all flesh is grass. The grass withers. The flowers fade. Only the word of the Lord (something more than human, something tied to the basic mystery of creation: why there is something rather than nothing) endures forever.

False prophets cry "peace, peace" when there is no peace. False counselors let us consider our marital troubles, or our cancer, or our financial woes apart from the big questions of worldwide suffering, certain aging, and death. Freud distinguished between the mental pains that can be cured and the hardships of life that must be accepted. For him mental health was the ability to love and to work, not the ability to escape pain or the capacity always to be happy. The deepest thing we can do for our practical troubles is to reconcile ourselves to the dark side of human existence, the surety of suffering. The most realistic mind-set we can bring to our problem of alcoholism or romantic heartbreak is a wry recognition that being in trouble is quintessentially human.

CHAPTER TWO

Feeling

OVERVIEW

WE CANNOT SEPARATE THOUGHTS AND FEEL-ings. Even scientists working in the labora-tory are moved by frustration with past ex-periments, enthusiasm for new hypotheses, the thrill of an elegant explanation, hope for worldwide recognition and fame. Still, it has seemed useful to focus first on the more in-tellectual side of our interior lives and then on the more emotional side. In this chapter we consider nine species of emotion or feel-ing.

First, we deal with *pain*. All troubles bring pain. To be suffering, hurting, is the common bond of people in trouble. Some pain is physical. More is emotional—feelings hurt, hopes dashed. But all pain is challeng-ing. Until we get a handle on it, find a way to lessen it or accept it, we are victims, people not in control. It is unpleasant to be a victim. Victimhood is hurtful in its own right. No doubt that is why people with AIDS don't want the label "victim," why some people who have suffered rape don't want it. It can seem to deepen their status as sufferers. It can remind them that they are or were helpless. Nonetheless, whether victims or not, they and all other people in trouble are bonded to suffering. Pain is the near side of their trouble, its constant calling card. So we begin with pain, taking up its sharp emotional challenge.

Second, we reflect on *fear*. Being afraid is itself painful (many phenomena and categories of the interior life overlap), but fear is different from muscle spasms, different even from regret or feeling foolish. We fear the future, because we can imagine more pain tomorrow and the next day. We fear finding ourselves without money or friends or any meaning to our lives. We fear we may never find another job, or another person with whom to share life, or another chance to convince our child we love her. And our fear takes away our happiness, threatens our peace, shrinks our capacity to love and to work. Our fear is seldom a friend, regularly an enemy. Until we can face it, at least ward it off, it can be a major part of our trouble.

Third, trouble can also bring something deeper: *anxiety*. Many psychologists distinguish between fear and anxiety. Where fear is tied to specific bad things that may happen, anxiety is free-floating. We are nervous, anxious, but we know not of what. We tremble at life, the future, the need to keep holding together a self. If we are philosophic, we may realize that our anxiety is tied to our nothingness, what philosophers call our contingency. There is no necessity in our being. We did not make ourselves, and we have no certain reason for being. We will pass out of being, it seems, at death, and death can come at any moment. Our shudders of anxiety reach down to these cracks in our foundations. Like waves of an earthquake, they come from a deep-seated fault.

Fourth, we can come to feel *helpless,* with or without great anxiety. We've tried this and that, come up empty, and so are tempted to feel nothing will ever succeed. This is victimhood with a vengeance. This is the worst of psychological states. Our trouble is overwhelming us. We have no energy to oppose to it, no hope of ever getting on top. Only if someone else lends a hand are we likely to turn the corner and begin the way back. Only if we finally hit rock bottom, confess our helplessness, and look outside for a stronger power are we likely to oppose our addiction. Because even people who struggle mightily with their troubles can feel helpless from time to time, any adequate survey of negative feelings must grapple with helplessness.

Fifth, we also have positive feelings, and one of

the most helpful is *confidence*. Confidence lets us expect to make progress. Confidence is the inner voice telling us we can do it, it is only a matter of time. Few people have an excess of self-confidence. Most of us need a pat on the back, a realistic bit of encouragement, at least once a week. Especially needy are people in the grip of serious trouble. The man or woman going through a trying divorce is likely to feel down and rattled. The woman or man who has lost a job is likely to feel filled with doubts. So building confidence in both the self and the human condition is always important. Helping people square their shoulders and take a deep breath can be the difference between their eventual success or failure.

Sixth, related to confidence is *courage*. When bad things happen, we ought to get angry and resolve to oppose them. Certainly, as noted in the last chapter, we finally have to make our peace with an imperfect world. But when trouble drifts in, we are right to get tough with ourselves, get angry with the troublemakers. We need energy to oppose what is threatening our home, our family, our peace of mind. Courage and anger can supply it. It is wrong to think that good people never get angry. Anger is the right, the necessary, reaction to injustice. When we see the rich making victims of the poor, ruining their lives, we ought to become furious with the rich and hate their wrongdoing. When we realize we have been told lies and pushed around, we ought to lash out at those who have mistreated us. We need what Paul Tillich called "the courage to be." From our own depths, and the help of our friends, we must summon the strength to keep going. When we do, no trouble need defeat us.

Seventh, if we feel *connected* to other people, and/or to more than human powers, we are in good shape to fight our troubles. This is a consideration that we develop fully in Chapter Three, when we deal with sharing our situation with friends and professional caregivers. It occurs here too, however, because it is a crucial feeling. Few things are more debilitating than feeling you are completely alone. Alone, you easily imagine your troubles to be insuperable. Connected to other people, you realize that they too know about alcoholism, or drug use, or depression, or violence and divorce. They too have been unhappy, maybe are unhappy right now. Moreover, they may take your troubles to heart, and so lessen them markedly. Through their sympathy, and their help in sharing practical tasks, they may whittle away at your sorrow. It is not good for man or woman to be alone. It is a great help to feel connected to others.

Eighth, when we feel that others *support* our struggles against trouble, we are likely to feel confidence, courage, and a half-dozen other positive emotions. Support, which intensifies connection, becomes substantial when we can rely on it through thick and thin. Indeed, support is a major reason for marriage: to share life in all circumstances, for better or worse, richer or poorer, in sickness or in health. Biblical Israel felt that its God had struck a covenant, formed a relationship with it that approximated a marriage. In all circumstances it could find God nearby, present as he chose to be. Indeed, Israel would learn the name of God, the nature of God, only by living with him over time like a spouse. So we find the Psalmist and many of the Prophets expecting God to support them. Analogously, we find mystics of all the religions insisting that their lives belong to God more than to themselves.

Ninth and last, we consider the fullest sort of positive emotion, a deep *trust* that surpasses even painful trouble—a trust in oneself, or in life, or in God. Because you feel that someone or something is holding you close, protecting you against despair and madness, you keep placing one foot before another. I knew a woman who had ten difficult children, the last born when she was fifty. She never lost her basic trust in the goodness of her life. She had the courage to kick out her philandering husband as soon as the youngest kid started school. Thirteen years later, when she found she had Parkinson's disease, she continued to possess her spirit in peace. She remains a marvel in my judgment, her trust something of a miracle. Through all her troubles she has never lost it. Frequently I struggle to match her.

PAIN

Three images of pain: First, a man cries out in agony, because his back muscles have gone into spasm again, due to crushed vertebrae. Second, a woman weeps and keeps saying, "I hate her, I hate her," as she recalls how her mother mistreated her in childhood. Third, another woman sobs at the loss of her husband to cancer. What will she do? Half of her self has gone missing.

Until he receives medicine to blunt his pain, the man with the back spasms can only roll in misery, wondering why he is being crucified. Until she can get her deep-seated fury out, the woman hating her mother can enter no balancing, qualifying judgments. The woman sobbing for the loss of her husband can only hope that time will prove healing. In her bones she knows she will never be whole again. She has loved completely, becoming one flesh with her man. Part of her will always feel torn, gone missing, a source of phantom pains.

Pain puts the sharpest edge on our troubles. When we writhe in physical or emotional agony, we call life hateful. Indeed, we do well if we refrain from calling God hateful: Who but a sadist would allow such suffering? Around the world millions of little children are starving, millions more live worse than

wild animals. Life is not pleasant, when we let ourselves see the enormities of human suffering. In ages
past, as in our own time, the powerful grind down
the weak. Disease and ignorance blight the lives of
the majority. "Reality" is not pretty.

One must be tough to face up to pain. Yet facing it is inevitable. It is right to feel that pain is
horrible, a thing accursed. It is wrong to be sure it
will defeat us. Sometimes physical pain is beyond our
handling. We can only hope the morphine will be
strong enough. Often emotional pain submits to loving attention. If others hold us, literally or symboli-
cally, they can rock away our worst hurts. The common wisdom is that time is the best healer, patience
our best friend. A year after the death of a spouse,
most widows or widowers are functioning adequately. Those who have been blessed with a profound love, a true marriage of spirits, know they will
never "recover." But for some a bond with the departed continues. The sharing has gone so deeply
that the voice of the deceased keeps speaking in
memory, sometimes most consolingly. Then pain
can yield to gratitude. Indeed, pain itself can seem
proof of love. Despite their tears, the survivors
would not have it otherwise.

We can only hope and pray that we too, and the
friends we see suffering, can reach this same judgment. Painful as our divorce or cancer or loss of a
child may be, we too can still desire to say we are

grateful we were born. Maybe the marriage had some good years before it turned sour. Maybe it gave us a couple of wonderful children. Maybe the cancer, however frightening, has come at a reasonable hour, when we feel the bulk of our life's work is done. Whatever, something in us remains grateful. The light of our eyes, the air we've breathed, has been grace.

I remember trying to console a couple whose child had just drowned at a picnic. One minute he was playing by the bank of the river; the next minute he was under the water and drowned. I had no words. All the pious phrases stopped in my throat. I could only weep with them and hold them. I could only ask God to carry them through. Sometimes that's our only option. Pain makes no sense and we're forced to fly blind. Life is far too dark for us, much too heavy. We can only wait for some lightening, groaning and moaning sorrowfully. Henri de Lubac once said that when we really suffer we do it badly. We are not graceful. There is no comeliness in us. We resemble a crucified God.

FEAR

Fear does not seem so formidable to me as pain, yet I don't doubt that it causes great suffering. People who live in the midst of violence, in terrible households or neighborhoods, dwell in an outpost of hell. People trapped in the midst of warfare, pawns in a brutal game, do well not to break from the strain. The various police states rule by fear, and all civilized people call their regimes despicable. Many of the mentally ill live in constant fear, whether of their own demons or of a God breathing fire.

So there is much suffering in the world from fear, a great cruelty. If we have not grown up in a secure family, protected by love and a minimal prosperity, we have begun life with a solid strike against us. The wonder is that so many of us survive unpromising beginnings. We carry deep scars, but we keep struggling to move forward.

One of the worst aspects of fear is that it can numb our emotions and paralyze us. Afraid, we can stay in the cross fire, unable to move forward or back. Sometimes we eventually realize that moving would cost less than staying stuck, but often we overcome the paralysis of fear only if others pull us out.

When afraid, we find it hard to credit our own voices. Like children lying in the dark, we need an outside assurance that no monsters will devour us. Friends do much good work by offering such assurance. If people we respect, and know care for us, say that we can successfully change jobs, or leave a sick household, or enter a rehabilitation program, we may hold our fears at bay long enough to give such options a try.

As soon as we begin to generate even a small pattern of success—two weeks completed at the new office or in the program of therapy—we have some evidence, some justification for staring down our fears. In the beginning, though, the assurances, the support, of our friends can make all the difference.

Many of my convictions about the therapies of the contemplative life root in the fact that I myself found it healing. For five years I lived in a monastic setting, able to sink deeply into quiet and make it my interior own. In that quiet much of the disease of a twisted upbringing lessened. The fever came down. The lesions cleared up. I let go of a lot of anger. I realized my parents were not much to blame. Their parents before them had been inadequate. The fathers had eaten sour grapes and the children's teeth were set on edge. How far back in time did it go?

Out of the world, away from the pathologies of home, my fears lessened. I began to realize that success was more than proving oneself. One day I sensed that I could just be, with no need for self-defense. In the depths of silence, thinking idly about the brevity of life and its great imperfection, I became grateful just to share it—just to know, however briefly, its solace and peace. How improbable that any of us should be here! What a miracle the genesis of our earth and its evolution! And what a further miracle that now and then we enjoy great beauty—even experience love.

Beauty and love are powerful antidotes to fear and sorrow. Sometimes a lovely day can give us a solid respite. Certainly, we have to work to remove the causes of fear and sorrow, whether physical or emotional. Naturally, we can't play Pollyanna with harsh realities. Still, we can hope that fearful people will enjoy some respites. We can try to bring them a touch of beauty, offer them at least a look of love.

Fearful people, sad people, people in trouble all need times when they are moved out of themselves. Yes, art, music, romance, even prayer are uncertain sources of ecstasy, never guaranteed. Nonetheless, each generation has reported that they are precious, because from time to time they can take us away. So I can only say, "Try them. Give yourself a day at the museum, a walk in the park, an hour of quiet, lovely music. Let your heart continue to hope for love, to want at least to believe in love. Tell your fears they are ugly, unwelcome, and you no longer will be their prisoner. Tell your friends you want their help, you are ready to tell them your story. A friend helped by a friend is like a strong city. A person able to look for beauty, to hope for love, to let go to interior silence is well advanced in the process of healing."

ANXIETY

Fear is a hardship but not unusual. Indeed, often it makes great sense: The life swirling outside can be something we ought to fear. Anxiety moves us a large step closer to pathology. When we are really anxious, we need more than our friends can supply. For we've sensed the profound fragility of all human existence, the deep crack in our foundations. Until someone can assure us that this is not fatal, we're likely to put our living on hold.

Who can give us such assurance? Our best poets ponder the deep cracks, often coming away shuddering. For example, T. S. Eliot's heroine Celia, the most interesting character in *The Cocktail Party,* senses that existence itself is flawed. If it were only she who had trouble coping, she who felt herself inadequate or a mess, the anxiety would be bearable. But to think that humanity itself, maybe even creation as well, has something profoundly wrong with it gives her the willies. That seems too much to face, so she asks the help of a psychiatrist.

We have only two significant options when we experience genuine anxiety. We can accept the assurances of people with some claim to authority, some mantle of wisdom, and trust that existence will hold together enough for us to make our way through our years, be they many or few. Or we can experience directly, for ourselves, forces more powerful than death, dissolution, nothingness, even evil. We can learn in our own minds and hearts that love or life or being or maybe sheer determination, simple cussedness, can preserve us.

The second option, direct personal experience, is the more powerful and trustworthy source of healing. Somehow, usually quite mysteriously, we hear a voice, typically speaking without words, that says with the medieval Christian mystic, Julian of Norwich, "All manner of thing shall be well." We can never prove to others that we have had this experience, let alone that we are wise to trust it. We can only know that it soothed our anxieties enough to result in a commitment. We discovered that we had the strength to keep going. We felt empowered to give our children, our spouse, our work, our God— or even ourselves—what was needed from us. How many people have this experience, I cannot say. However, when I think of those I have seen come back from despair, I have to believe it happens more than occasionally.

The spectacular cases are people like George Fox, founder of the Quakers, who came back from the far side of desperation, from a terrible anxiety about his selfhood and worth, riding the winds of a powerful conviction. The psychologist Erik Erikson, looking for the source of the unusual power shown by such world-shaking figures as the Mahatma Gandhi, believed that typically such people had looked through, moved through, the darkness that terrifies most of us and, strangely, had drawn strength from it. As though the worst possibilities had run their course, and they found themselves still surviving, thereafter the Gandhis and Foxes showed no fear. When the English religious establishment put him in jail, George Fox did not care. When the British put him in jail, Gandhi did not care. What were human jails compared to the prisons, the hellish dungeons, of the spirit, from which both men had escaped?

If the people who persuade us to let go of our anxieties and entrust ourselves to life know their business, they have based their case on extraordinary individuals like Fox and Gandhi. Ideally, they have also tested these deep waters for themselves, according to their own need and courage. The point to the hagiography, the traffic in lives of the saints, that one finds in all the major religious traditions is to assure later believers that the pathway they are traveling has been well trod before them. Others have managed to make it through. The point to smaller-gauged sharing with counselors or friends is to gather honest evidence that others are still finding life possible.

So the argument becomes, "If they can do it, why can't I?" When "they" convince us that they are not markedly brighter or stronger than we, and that they were at least as badly off, we have to take this argument seriously. Finally hitting the bottom, they wept their way through despair and let go. They knew they were powerless. They had to surrender to something greater than themselves. And this something greater also seemed greater than the cracks, the nothingness, in the foundations of creation. It seemed a universal power of healing, available to all whose self-sufficiency broke under their need.

I can't guarantee that the trouble signaled by "anxiety" will always yield to the breaking of self-sufficiency. I have no control over that sort of power, no ability to dispense it right or left. I can only say that history is full of uncanny stories. Not all the people brought to the brink tumble over. Some return stronger than they were before. Maybe you can be one of their number. Maybe there is more than threat in your life as well.

HELPLESSNESS

When we feel helpless, whether from anxiety or weakness or loneliness, we are stuck in our troubles. We can see no way out, so we curl up to await the worst. Still, we are never completely helpless. There are at least two distinct ways of letting go.

One is negative, closing ourselves to any future possibility of change. The other is positive: "Things have passed out of my hands, but maybe my hands are not the only factors."

Once I dealt with a young mother withered by the divorce action of her husband. He had left her for a younger, brighter model, and her self-esteem was scraping bottom. Moreover, her church frowned on divorce and allowed no possibility for remarriage. So she was suffering a double whammy. Who would want her, if the father of her children could reject her? And how could she think of a fresh start, when her church said remarriage would make her hateful to God?

I liked to look at this woman, because she was very pretty. But I also did not like to look, because most of what I saw was pain. Her children, two handsome boys, seemed to me fierce accusers of her husband. The Valium she was taking to muffle her pain left her dull and feeling helpless. I remember telling her three things, all of which I believed completely. The first was that her husband (tall, handsome, smart, and self-centered) was a jerk, pure and simple. She might doubt that, and so blame herself, but I had met him, and I knew her, so I had no doubt: jerk, pure and simple.

The second thing I told her was that she was very pretty, and a wonderful mother—both just plain truths. Unless I knew very little about men, she was not going to lack their attention. I could not guarantee that most of those paying her attention would not also be jerks, but I thought at least a few might be worth knowing.

Third, I told her that I thought the current policy of her church was not the final word. Other churches had different policies, supposedly drawn from the same teachings of Jesus. Moreover, her church allowed more exceptions than she realized—many of its wealthy had long managed annulments. So perhaps her future was not so closed as she tended to think. Perhaps in a year or so, when she had healed, she would make a new beginning. Initially she did not believe me, but three years later, when she had remarried with most of her self-confidence and hope restored, she thought I was a genius.

I have other stories, naturally, and many do not end so happily. I know more than one graduate student who got lost in self-doubts and never got his dissertation finished. I know more than one divorced woman who never remarried. None of these people has remained precisely helpless. All have picked up and moved on, piecing together a new life. Though their failures continue to dog them, bad experiences have not rendered them helpless. Once I feared that they would. Once their future seemed dismal. But in fact they proved more resilient than I imagined.

Thinking about helplessness, the times I've worried about people's future, I've come to suspect that many of us are tougher than we realize. Not all of us. For various reasons some of us are fragile and break tragically. But the majority of us nurse our wounds and regain some measure of health, enough to return to the battle. In our bodies and spirits, below our full knowing, lie unquenchable desires for life.

Eric Voegelin, a great philosopher of history, has said that human beings will not live by depravity alone. Contemplating the spiritual horrors wrought by Nazism and Marxism, he found in the human spirit a profound will to resist. The recent revolution in Eastern Europe, though occurring after Voegelin's death in 1986, vindicated his belief. Despite the ugly upheavals that tore apart Yugoslavia, the victories of spirit won in the former Soviet Union and other long-Communist lands of Eastern Europe prove that many people will always keep battling for the truth.

Why not the same in the personal sphere? Why not a congenital will to resist humiliation, to reject apparent meaninglessness, to fight on to live in the light? When you feel helpless, ask your spirit, your inmost self, whether you really are ready to surrender. Your spirit may well tell you that as long as there is still something good that you love, or something evil that you hate, the time to quit has not yet come.

CONFIDENCE

When we feel pain, fear, anxiety, helplessness, or any of the many other negative emotions, our sense of value and possibility shrinks. We believe we are not worth much and have little future. On the other hand, when we feel confidence, courage, and the other positive states of emotion, our being expands, many more things seem possible. The etymological roots of "confidence" suggest a faith and strength that bring us together. The roots of "courage" suggest a great heartening. What can we do to invite or reinforce these beneficial feelings?

We can note, first, that people give one another confidence. No one can give us confidence that is unshakable, but our parents and teachers, our lovers and friends, can help us mightily. If they believe in us, we find it easier to believe in ourselves. When they are standing by us, we ourselves tend to stand taller. Many children venture into adolescence and adulthood gracefully only because their parents have given them the momentum. Many spouses try their new business, or stand up to their bosses, or hang on through sharp criticism only because the person sharing their life most intimately is sure they are right. In the beginning confidence tends to draw strength from others. It becomes secure, however, stable, only when we can supply it on our own.

Self-confidence is not arrogant or overweening. It is simply an interior strength that experience has taught us is justified. Because we have done well in school in the past, we are confident we will do well at the next level. Because we have handled tough accounts well in the past, we don't worry when a new challenge comes our way. Naturally, people in trouble seldom feel so secure. Self-confidence may be precisely what they are lacking. It has gone out the window with their recent failure. Their divorce, or relapse into depression, or new addiction to alcohol tells them daily that they should not be confident. They should doubt their every first inclination, because they have screwed things up so royally. A lot of therapy, therefore, goes toward rebuilding self-confidence, self-esteem, conviction that one is more than a screwup.

Happy the troubled person who can call on a solid friend or counselor at this juncture. Blessed the outside person, strong and objective, who can help put a troubled person's difficulties in perspective. A failed marriage is a miserable experience, but it does not justify the complete ruin of your confidence. Struggling with depression is bound to make you feel rotten, a loser at life, but in fact, matters are more complicated. A great many successful people have had to battle through depression. First-rank artists and leaders seem nearly certain to have experienced it. Even I, a fairly sunny lightweight, have found myself down in the dumps from cancer. If we are minded to look at either reality or ourselves squarely, we are bound to see a great deal that is depressing.

But that will seldom be the whole story. Almost always we will have overlooked significant strengths, achievements, reasons to think well of ourselves and feel blessed. Good counselors excel at righting the balance in this way. Good friends never let us get too down on ourselves. If we listen to either, we can start to gain objectivity in our own right. We can start to realize that though our weaknesses are many, we have significant strengths on which we can rely. Maybe we have continued to hold our job, even continued to do it well. Or maybe we have raised our children well, despite significant reverses. Or maybe we have battled courageously against a serious disease, impressing many outsiders. Any of these achievements is good grounds for self-confidence.

Ultimately, the best grounds is the simple fact that we are as we have been made. This is our personality, our intellectual endowment, the emotional kit we have inherited. We have to accept it, even love it, because the alternative is unthinkable. To reject ourselves, hate the way we have been made, is to say no to things far beyond us. We did not make ourselves. That we are as we are is part of the great scheme of creation. If we hate the great scheme of creation, we are always swimming against the tide. Creation will always defeat us. We did not give the seas their boundaries. We were not the ones who hung the stars. We had no say in designing our genetic inheritance.

So we must trust that greater powers are at work in creation, and that this work embraces ourselves. Otherwise we shall go mad with useless railings. Otherwise we shall hate the fact that we are not God. Amusingly, the fact that we are not God can be a profound source of self-confidence. We don't have to be God, only the selves we have been made. It does not matter how others judge us. If we are true to these selves, we can feel strongly satisfied.

COURAGE

It takes courage to keep on going, even in the most apparently easy life. It takes grit to become mature, whole, possessed of anything approaching wisdom. Athletes are always speaking of growing through "adversity," and their speech says more than they know. While I hesitate to call losing a ball game "adversity," I agree that dealing with failure can build character. Again and again one hears from successful writers that they had to endure many rejections. From near and far the report tends to be that important things in life become clear only through trial and error.

Courage is the heart to keep trying, even when one has tasted bitter failure. Courage is a great help, therefore, in times of significant trouble. Where those without courage tend to cave in to crippling disease, the courageous are likely to keep fighting. Better life in a wheelchair than no life at all. Better a staggering walk, won through hard hours of rehabilitation, than being confined to a wheelchair. The more determined we are to fight our troubles tooth and nail, the more likely we are to triumph over them. The shrewder our friends and family, the more quickly they will encourage us to such fight.

Often I've realized that the basic concerns of my life are all self-justifying. My work, my love of my wife, and my prayer regularly feed my courage, my joy in going on. I can be discouraged, wondering whether I'll ever again feel I have something to say, but the process of writing reassures me: Nowhere else do I see such visions. I can wonder whether the future, clouded now by cancer, won't be unbearably grim, but a word from my wife about living in the present will set me straight again. When I enter the quiet and darkness of prayer, accepting that God is too much for me, almost always I experience a resetting of my priorities. Most of my agenda doesn't matter. Keeping faith, holding hope, and continuing to love are enough.

People in trouble can look to their work, the loves in their lives, and their prayer to see whether these central concerns give them life, courage, strength to go on. If they do not, it is time to reassess them. The first rule, spoken deep into our animal nature, is that we must try to survive. If the work we do, the friends with whom we associate, and the ways we deal with life's mysteriousness are not supporting us, it is time to overhaul them. We need new work, more creative or better geared to help other people. We need new friends, or a new depth in our relations with old ones. And we need a new philosophy or religion, a better way of contacting the ultimate questions and mysteries. It is time to move along, spiritually, because we are stagnating. Our lack of heart, strength, zest, tells us we've become captives.

So get out into the night, the exodus from slavery. Get out into something new, more deeply breathed, closer to creativity and freedom. Bestir yourself, troubled person. Take yourself in hand. You can do more than you give yourself credit for. You have more courage than you think.

CONNECTION

With his little exhortations, an author like me is trying to make connection. Despite the difficulty of the printed page, a writer wants to create a tie. You, gentle reader, are the doppelgänger moving along with me on every page. Without your presence in my head, my writing would have no objective intention. I would not be trying to bore ahead, clearing a tunnel for you. My work would be only practice, scales and riffs to keep myself in shape. Even as solitary a work as writing is intrinsically social. Even the most mute of our prayers begs God's mercy on the entire world.

What I am calling "connection" is this intrinsically social human nature we carry. For the matter of dealing with trouble, it has moment hard to overestimate. In the first place, many of our troubles come from other people. Our parents, or friends, or spouses, or lovers, or children figure mightily in our nightmares, our daydreams, our pains. We feel responsible for them, so we have no choice but to hoist some of their burdens. Their troubles intertwine with ours; we cannot separate neatly where their pains leave off and our own begin.

Even the sick, who we might think can locate their troubles quite precisely (heart disease here, stomach cancer there, nervous exhaustion the third bed over), do not suffer or worry alone. Few feelings are worse than that of being a burden to others. Few worries are more vexing than that of draining the family's financial resources, or causing others constant worry, or seeing in others' eyes an anger at being abandoned. To suffer alone would be trying, but it would not carry temptations to guilt—we might lash our body for having let us down, but we would not then lash ourselves for letting down people we love. Yes, even those enduring, more or less patiently, in private rooms often carry social burdens. Even old people, who have spent themselves for others, can worry that their last days are spoiling things for their daughters or sons.

The other side of our social nature, though, is the help we give one another. Step back some time and think about the organization of a hospital, or a college, or a synagogue, or even an insurance company. It is remarkable that human beings have cooperated to build such institutions for the common good. It is worth a long reflection, and many cheers. Who brought together all these doctors, nurses, support people? Who built the buildings, gathered the dazzling modern equipment, staffed the pharmacy, raised the money? More interestingly, why did they do it? What kept them going through all the frustrations, moved them across all the obstacles? It is not enough to say that they hoped to make money.

Much more central was their will to help, to heal, to cure, to console. Most people enter medicine because they feel a talent and desire to be healers. They may compromise this idealism as they grow older, but a remarkable social orientation usually remains. Their lives make no sense apart from serving other people. Their gamble is that helping the needy justifies their time.

The needy have to learn to depend on this altruism. They have to test the desire of others to help, and find it solid. When they do—when their acceptance of aid is not just a reflex, or a necessity they may bitterly regret later on—they may suspect what many children sense quite accurately: Adults carry an important need to be needed. Helping those in pain, alleviating trouble, is by no means a one-way street. The majority of adults need to be parents and teachers. Deep in our psyches works a strong desire to pass on what we have learned. This desire connects the generations. If people in middle age did not instinctively want to run the institutions on which society depends, we would lapse back toward tribal cultures.

Sometimes it is good for people to be alone, to taste solitude. Sometimes that is the best way to hear the still, small voice that does not sound in the storm or the crowd. But seldom is it good for us to feel lonely, abandoned, without family and friends, unconnected. People caught in the grip of negative emotions need few things more than connection.

Let a friend appear with a kind word, a patient ear, and usually some healing begins. Let the social reality of the situation reemerge, the parameters set by family, work, friends, and other objective markers, and usually the practical tasks implied in the trouble become clearer. When we get lost in imagination, our fears run rampant and our courage goes AWOL. As soon as we reconnect ourselves to the outside world, coping becomes prosaic and possible.

SUPPORT

"Connection" brings to mind a network, a circle of friends or allies, and so it connotes support. "Support," however, is a stronger concept. Only when the members of our family or our friends get behind us, lifting us up with their different kinds of help, should we speak of significant support. Only when we find allies who are doers, not just talkers or emoters, is our sense of isolation and helplessness likely to lessen. Many more people wish us well than take the time, make the effort, to do something specific, concrete, sacrificial to help us. Their wishes are welcome, but those we later call lifesavers are the ones who rolled up their sleeves.

Once we had some friends who became hard-pressed financially. The father lost his job to physical disability. The kids were moving from a tuition-free

high school to pricey colleges. Many friends and
family members felt great sympathy and showed it. A
few dug down and sent money, actual cash. The
many were not useless or hypocritical. The few,
however, made the real difference. Certainly, our
friends and family usually have limited resources.
They cannot dole out money, or even large amounts
of time, for every good cause that comes their way.
But if we have no family members or friends able to
help us practically, we are bound to feel isolated—set
adrift on an ice floe with no one the sadder.

Once the tribe was bound to care for its own.
Even today newcomers to our country, immigrants
from foreign lands, tend to look to one another for
support. What seems clannishness may be merely
tried ways of saving the family. Much in the originally Confucian ethic of honoring one's parents,
spending oneself completely for the family, explains
the drive of Asian-Americans—for example, why so
many succeed as students of the natural sciences. The
fracture of family life among African-Americans
shows us the reverse of this natural instinct. While a
great many African-Americans sustain strong family
ties, the ruin of family life in the ghettos shows the
long arms of slavery and prejudice.

Among the religious communities, support is
also important. All the groups that think of themselves as God's "people" offer high reasons for char-
ity and practical help. Look at the leading private

agencies for social help. Look at the history of phi-
lanthropy in this country. Although the religious
groups have not succeeded in keeping the wealthy
from gouging the poor, they have spurred many
wealthy people to give great sums to charitable
causes. One can debate the political wisdom of this
arrangement. The case for a socialist government
seems strong to most idealistic people, until one
looks at how such a government tends to work out
in practice. Nonetheless, even to debate the wisdom
of a massive change in our system for health care, or
for how we get aid to dependent children, or for
how we finance research on AIDS is to affirm the
connections among us. Even to say we should do
better is to affirm the legitimacy of every suffering
person's outcry for help.

So if you are a person in deep trouble, you are
right to look for support. Should your family not
supply it, look to your friends. Should your friends
prove inadequate, look to religious groups, government agencies, private charities. It may be that all
your looking will be futile, but chances are it will
not. Chances are, if you keep knocking on door after
door, one of them will open.

My friend, the local head of Planned Parent-
hood, comes to mind at this juncture. In three years
she has doubled the resources available to all people,
but especially to the poor, who want help with family planning, prenatal care, the cure of sexually trans-

mitted diseases. Next on her agenda is a program for "well-babies": postnatal care up to seven years. She is a dynamo, and unusual, but every city has a few like her. If you are in trouble, they are the type you want to find.

Moreover, my friend gets help. Though the United Way does not cooperate fully, she has managed to raise millions from private sources. This also is not unusual. In most cities at least a few wealthy citizens are willing to help provide prenatal services, housing for the indigent, shelters for the homeless. Because they think of the city as their home, they want to support programs to improve it. Above all, they want to help people they consider less fortunate. Forget the condescension their attitude can carry. Forget the radical social reforms necessary to reduce the ranks of the unfortunate—reforms that many wealthy people would oppose. Simply accept the fact that support, like everything else in politico-social life, reflects an imperfect system. Simply be grateful that this church, or that welfare agency or private benefactor, is glad to be of help, gratified to support you in your struggles.

TRUST

The best feeling a person in trouble can experience is that of trust. Trust allows us to expect support, to lean on it and take risks because of it. We are fortunate when we can trust other people. Our self-confidence peaks when we can trust ourselves. And the depths of a mature trust amount to giving a blank check to providence. Somehow we take the risk of believing that all things serve a grand plan.

It is hard for people whose parents have failed them to develop a mature trust. It is hard for them even to trust other people. If the ones first entrusted with their care have let them down, why should people with lesser ties stay faithful? The only way to cut across this vicious question is to show the distrustful a truly selfless love. The rare people we call saints specialize in this love. The rest of us manage it only occasionally. Nonetheless, now and then someone loves me, and works for my benefit, without much need of recompense. The good deed alone is pay enough. The gratitude I cannot keep from my face is sufficient compensation.

Have you a parent or spouse or child whose love is truly unflagging? Is there a friend you can call at any hour? If you do, if there is, you know volumes about trustworthiness. As well, you know how you yourself ought to respond, when the call comes to you to go and do likewise. Once we were returning from Kansas City to Wichita in our little Volkswagen when we lost power. Night had fallen and we felt terribly alone. Car after car went zooming by. We had no way even to call a road service. Finally one car stopped, backed up, and offered us a ride to the turnoff. When it turned out that was not enough, the man took us to a nearby motel and waited while we made arrangements for towing. Later we learned he was a fundamentalist Christian. We stood so deeply in his debt that I felt obliged to reread the parable of the Good Samaritan (Luke 10), pondering my obligation to go and do likewise.

Is it mere psychological blather to investigate whether people in trouble tend not to trust themselves, or are all human beings bound to feel trustworthy? My sense is that many people do not trust themselves. They feel weak, inadequate, unprepared. Or they fear they will lose control, become angry and irrational. The more trouble they have known, the less likely they are to trust they will manage well in new crises. Each failure has increased their tendency to feel gun-shy. Each need to call on others for money or comfort has increased their sense of dependence. Whatever we can do to boost their self-confidence is bound to feed their trust in themselves. The pity is that by the time we meet many, their distrust is deep and long-standing.

I had a friend who did many things well but never seemed able to reveal herself, give herself away completely, as passionate love requires. She was confident in her work. She trusted her audiences would applaud. But she shied away from the depths of her selfhood, where there was a past and some character traits she feared. Who would she be if her immaculate appearance was rumpled? How could she be sure she'd be accepted if people knew her "real" self? So she could never be fully honest, and her relations could never get deep. Her smile remained ready and pleasing, but often it was tinged with sadness. She paid a high price for not trusting herself, and for not trusting those who wanted to love her. She remained alone, miserably alone, when she might have shared warmth better than wine.

When we look in the mirror, or when we examine our consciences, or when we brave the eye of providence, what do we find? Have we come to grips with our shortcomings? Does it still matter that we know others wiser, richer, better looking, more virtuous? As we come in sight of our finale, when the days to death are fewer than those back to birth, it is crucial that such things should not matter. Our lives have been what they had to be. After the fact, they seem nearly inevitable. This is not completely true, of course, because, when the two roads diverged in the yellow wood, we were in fact free. But with time the road not taken becomes irrelevant. It is what had to be, what we see now we had no way of avoiding, that is truly interesting.

For what had to be is the hand of fate in our story, the finger of God. Had we not developed the drinking problem, we would never have fallen apart and needed grace that became amazing. Had we kept our family together, we would have felt better about ourselves, but now our consolation is having nothing of which to boast, seeing the completeness of grace.

Admittedly, few people in our culture talk in these terms. One needs to go to the East, or to medieval writers, to find such brooding about gain and loss. When did biblical Israel truly prosper, in the desert or in the promised land? Why did the Christ have to suffer to enter his glory, as the Gospel of Luke seems to require? As Socrates went to his death by poison, was he more or less blessed than the hypocrites who had condemned him? When the Buddha sat nearly naked under the Bo-Tree, how could he be the richest of men?

Any answer to these paradoxical questions requires a clear sense of what is genuine success and what merely passing. Any deep sense of trust about the human venture, even the human necessity to experience trouble, requires us to let go of what the mob calls gain and content ourselves with emptiness.

Can it be that we must lose our lives to find them? Can trouble actually become our friend? Now and then I've found myself thanking my myeloma. It doesn't last, but for the moment I feel held by something dazzling. Would that I might always trust it.

CHAPTER THREE

Sharing

OVERVIEW

WE HAVE CONSIDERED HOW TO THINK ABOUT trouble and how to sift feelings. Now we move outside the self, to how to share your troubles with others. As with the prior considerations, we cannot be exhaustive. Nonetheless, by the time you've finished with this chapter, you may know more about sharing than you did at the start.

Once again, the chapter takes up nine topics. First is sharing with your *family*—the parents, siblings, spouse, children, and wider relatives connected to you by blood. Blood is thicker than water, but often more troubled. What might seem the easiest sharing can be the hardest. So we may as well begin at the beginning. How can we open our hearts to those best poised not only to console us but also to wound?

101

Second, there is sharing with our *friends*. Actually, a good definition of a "friend" is one with whom we can share—both good things and bad. Ideally, such sharing is spontaneous, natural, something we barely reflect upon. In practice things may not be so simple. Our friends are more or less ideal. Our competition with them, our trust of them, is more or less intense.

Third, what about sharing our troubles with *counselors?* At what point ought we to seek professional advice? If we do, what may we reasonably expect of it? Most of the counseling we are likely to seek will focus on our feelings. Are you ready to make your feelings known to a stranger? How are you going to evaluate what he or she suggests?

Fourth, many people take their troubles to their *clergy*—minister, priest, or rabbi. If he or she is a respected figure in the community, that can seem a wise choice. But what does a religious orientation tend to add to counseling? What sort of sharing do clergy expect to receive? There is no single answer to these questions, but they are worth considering before you knock on the door of a religious figure of authority.

Fifth, we may feel inclined to approach revered *teachers* with our troubles. If a person has impressed us in the classroom as smart, competent, and caring, we may think that he or she will be the same in the office. Often this proves true. What we saw in the classroom is what we get in the office. Still, it behooves us to remember we are not approaching a psychologist. From teachers we tend to get a blend of detached reason and common sense, rich in the measure that they are experienced—that they have suffered a bit themselves.

Sixth, we may feel inclined to approach a competent, kindly *physician,* all the more so if our trouble entails sickness or questions of health. Once again we are likely to find ourselves dealing with an authority figure who is not specifically trained in psychology. This does not mean that he or she cannot give us good counsel. It does mean that we probably should look for human traits more than specifically professional expertise.

Seventh, I throw in the category of *authors,* to suggest the sharing we can have with books. Certainly, this sharing tends to move in one direction, from the author to us. On the other hand, inasmuch as a book, an author, stimulates reflection, helps us get a good interior dialogue going, we can learn a great deal about our trouble. Whereas living conversations generally move quickly, with books we can linger to ponder and ruminate. Much of the best counsel I've received has come from my favorite authors. The classics of spirituality East and West stand among my greatest benefactors.

Eighth, I find it interesting to consider sharing trouble with *children.* How do we deal honestly with kids, who may or may not seem to need to know? If we have to go into the hospital, what should we tell a ten-year-old, especially one who already knows something's wrong? If loss of a job has reduced the family's resources drastically, how should we explain the constraints we must impose on our teenager's wardrobe, recreation, traveling? These can be painful questions, but we owe our children good answers. When we manage to work them out, trouble can occasion precious, even crucial, sharing.

Last, there is the matter of sharing with *God,* which can become relevant for more people than those who attend church or synagogue. When bad things happen to good people, it is natural to ask why of the ultimate powers. I believe we can get answers to our most troubling questions, but seldom in the way we initially desire. The mystery of life, the mystery of God, is always inviting our contemplation. The better we respond, the more congenial contemplation becomes, the more likely we are to leave a session of questioning recollected in spirit, knit back together in peace.

FAMILY

By happenstance my family was visiting when I got my diagnosis of cancer. I found this both good and bad—more good than bad, in the long run. Im-

mediately it was good because they could see for
themselves my physical condition, and also the first
impact of the news upon me. In the long run it was
good because they could build on those initial images, altering them as later news, fresher reports, required. But it was also bad because I had to see the
worry in their eyes, feel the pain in their hearts. I
could not avoid the fact that I was complicating their
lives as well as my own.

We never outgrow our primary relationships.
To the day we die we are the children of so and so,
our mother, so and so, our father. They have marked
us, for good and bad, in the most crucial period. By
the time we are five, much that we shall always be
has been stamped into our souls. From them we have
our basic biological endowment. They have given us
our first, archetypal sense of what it means to be
female and male. We are extremely fortunate if they
were wise, good, loving. We started life with a great
handicap if they were stupid, twisted, cold.

What can most of us share with our parents?
Usually less than we might like, more than we first
think. By the time that we have adult troubles, we
tend to realize that our parents are more like us than
not. Most of the time they are neither great saints
nor great sinners, neither special sages nor outstand-
ing fools. On the whole, they are likely to have our
well-being at heart. On the whole, we can approach
them for both counsel and practical aid. Even when

they cannot do much for us, it tends to be good to inform them.

My mother, nearly seventy-nine, took the news of my cancer well. She has lived long enough to know that all life is fragile. She has seen that bad news can be put to various uses. What I make of my cancer is as important as the fact that it has struck me. So I find that she listens more than she offers pep talks. Through our regular Sunday-morning calls, the bond between us has strengthened. I count that an unexpected benefit. For that alone I have to say multiple myeloma has not been all bad.

Closer than mother or father, though, is our spouse, the one for whom we have left mother and father, the one with whom we've been trying to become one flesh. Who can count all the ties, the crisscrossings, that time creates between spouses? Who can discern what houses and kids, good luck and bad, have woven from year after year? My sickness belongs to my wife as much as to me. It affects her life just as profoundly. If I could not share it with her, it and I would be very different. That I must share it with her, that it must slash her soul too, is perhaps my worst suffering. We partake in one fate. Deeper than money, work, divergent interests, mine is hers and hers is mine. Both blessing and curse, this marriage of selves is a primal reality. Each day I shake my head in wonder that her love is so strong.

You can imagine the further possibilities with family members. My ties with my sister are close, so she shares my current troubles intimately. My nephew and niece have a new cloud on their horizon, and with it a host of new questions. I count myself lucky to have no painful, alienated familial relations. When I look at people in trouble who do have familial relations already painful, I sense that their troubles feel multiplied. Sometimes hard times overcome estrangement. Other times they do not. If siblings have broken with one another bitterly, not even a mortal illness necessarily will set things right. If parents and children still have work of reconciliation waiting, they are wise to seize a time of trouble as a great opportunity—their last, for all they know.

One need not be religious to know that estrangement from family members is a special burden on one's conscience. True, none of us asked to have x for a sister or y for a father. On the other hand, having x or y is part of the providence we have to come to grips with, if we are not to hate the actual life we've been handed. True again, important things in our lives depend on our free choices. Who we've become was not all laid out before we were born. On the other hand, whom we've been given as blood relations in life should seem more than incidental. Unless human time is completely absurd, we're meant to ponder primal relations and take them to heart. If a time of trouble, ours or a close relative's, moves us to do this, we may call it in part redeemed.

FRIENDS

When we think of sharing, friends' may well be the faces that first come to mind. As noted, a friend is precisely someone with whom we can share good times and bad—someone with whom we want to share what most concerns us. Therefore, a friend is also someone who gives us relief. Sharing our troubles tends to cut them in half. Simply by getting them off our chest, making them part of the objective world, we reduce greatly their power to haunt us. The person listening to our troubles, taking our upset to heart, seems to accept part of our burden. For the moment we are not staggering under it alone. For the moment it has become part of the common fund of human suffering and so less idiosyncratic, less our unique shame.

Trouble is shameful. Perhaps I should have made more of that when discussing feelings. To be in debt, or abandoned by a husband, or told one no longer has a job makes the deep soul blush. A true friend minimizes our sense of shame. Instinctively, he or she stands with us, and so we no longer feel singled out. I remember listening to a friend expose some of his heartache at having no job. When I reminisced about my experience of getting fired, and then visiting the unemployment office each week, his eyes grew round. He had not known I had been there before him. My words of comfort, my counsel of patience and fighting self-doubt, carried a ring of authority and made him feel less ashamed.

Friends convey the impression that they have been there before us, or that but for the grace of God they could well have been. They are not immaculate or saintly. What has happened to us could happen to them—perhaps has happened more than once. So we stand together as equals. There is no temptation to profit from a good friend's pain. Rather, that pain aches in our own spirit. If there were any way we could, we would take it away and bear it ourselves. We know the goodness of our friend, and also his or her weakness. We feel that it is unfair that our friend should have to suffer. So we curse or pray, as is our bent, asking the fates to change things. We resolve, in a mood of concern, to keep a close eye on this dear person now suffering, lest she or he fall into depression and risk even greater harm.

The stereotype is that women are better at sharing than men. By and large I find this stereotype verified. Women may compete or jockey for position but usually less vigorously than men. Usually, women give and take openness, vulnerability, as coin of their realm. Only a few men manage anything comparable. In superb male friendships both parties have made themselves vulnerable, but superb male friendships, in contrast to good working relationships or arrangements for play, are depressingly rare.

I count myself unusual to number half-a-dozen male friends I could call at any hour, tell anything, ask for any favor knowing they feel the same. These friendships go back to an unusual time in our mid-twenties when we lived together in all-male monastic settings. Like marines or refugees bonded by intense challenges and need of one another, we fused in ways that dozens of years and thousands of miles have not washed away. Most men do not fuse in this way. Few men know one another's souls intimately.

Sometimes mature men and women can forge fine friendships, managing their heterosexual attractions so that a meeting of minds, a support of spirits, remains the central focus. Indeed, some men reveal themselves only to sympathetic women, their wives in the first instance but female friends in the second. As long as the women don't baby the men or let the men take them for granted, this arrangement can be useful. However, if it is to produce a genuine friendship, it has to become two-way—the men must become as able to listen and support as the women.

To listen and support—that is not a bad description of friendship. The classical Greek definition of the love expressed in friendship *(philia)* located its essence in sameness of mind. Friends were those who thought alike, could share constructive discourse. This is an interesting definition, but our time requires something rounder. For us good friends hear one another, even when they do not agree completely. As well, they offer a stable affection. We need warmth, as well as light. Less rational than the classical Greeks, our friends may be simpler and more human.

In the final analysis, friendship is a species of love, the most central human act. We should never forget this. If we get across to our friends that we really love them, we accomplish the main mission. Even if we don't understand, or agree, or know what to do practically, our love can supply the essence of support, can enable the essence of sharing. Indeed, the essence of help in time of trouble is beating away terrible loneliness. Help is well at work when troubled people feel someone is standing by them, not laughing or blaming but grieving as they do. Real trouble hurts terribly, and real friends hurt with us. Call it *com*passion, *con*dolence, *sym*pathy—all the apt words stress *with*. Indeed, following some German philosophers we might speak of friendship as a *Mitsein*—a being-with the other, an overlapping of selves. A famous saying has it that my friend is half of my soul. My wife meets that definition, and she has halved all my troubles.

COUNSELORS

We cannot expect counselors to be our friends, and yet to succeed, they have to do at least some of what friends do. By profession they are supposed to be people who understand emotional upset and can help us sort out our feelings. The assumption is that the tangle of our feelings is a large part of our trouble and pain. We have not been thinking straight or well, so we have gotten ourselves into bad places. We have not been feeling good about ourselves or our lives, so we have become woefully unhappy. More or less knowingly, we go to counselors to change things. If we are fortunate, we find people well enough trained, prudent enough, and kind enough to be helpful.

Like a good friend, a good counselor mainly listens. The listening, though, is active—a moving along with us that helps us clarify what we really think and feel. Much of the counselor's task is to enable us to find our own way and make our own decisions. The counselor cannot make important decisions for us. His or her job is to free us to decide for ourselves. Many counselors espouse a policy of not-judging. This may be hard to carry out in practice, but in theory they are working only to help us clarify our own judgments and values, not to impose what they think.

My main problem with the typical counselor is a reluctance to deal with mysteries. Few have anything to say about the great questions of evil and suffering, God and redemption. Almost by definition these questions fall outside their horizon, are not of practical interest. Yet I find that only the most prosaic troubles fit into an unmysterious framework. As soon as any significant pain or self-doubt comes on the scene, huge questions arrive willy-nilly. Not to admit them, or to profess oneself unable to deal with them, seems to me a confession of incompetence. But then I have not gone to many counselors, perhaps because I've intuited that our pheromones would clash and create a storm about life's mysteries.

I have no right to discourage people from seeking ordinary counseling, and I'm seldom happier with religious counseling. One might expect the latter to be competent to deal with life's mysteries. Unfortunately, the majority of so-called "pastoral counseling" seems to me half-baked humanistic psychology.

Still, I'm haunted by Jung's conviction that he never treated a person in the second half of life whose basic problems were not religious. Jung did not mean that his patients were disturbed by questions of doctrine or morality. He meant that they were suffering in the throes of finding the meaning of their lives, as the approach of death made such meaning ever more pressing. I have the impression that few American counselors are comfortable with an assertion like Jung's. Most find matters of deeper meaning, ultimate purpose, extremely dicey.

For example, even so sensitive an investigator as Robert Coles put off the study of children's dealings with ultimate questions until late in his harvest of interviews. His recent book, *The Spiritual Life of Children,* came some years after books on children's political and moral lives, long after *Children of Crisis,* his five volumes on how children coped with the racial and cultural upheavals of the 1960s.

Nonetheless, all power to counselors who can alleviate any degree of their counselees' pain, and full honors to any who can make their counselees happy and functional. Not all problems demand a deep analysis of their existential roots. Not every addiction or inability to handle money or failure to raise children well requires tracing a flight from life's mysteries. In some cases it is enough to get people to live by what we call common sense—ordinary shrewdness and prudence. It is significant progress if they agree that they should not spend more than they earn, should not trust smooth-talking sharpies. Once burned, they should remain twice shy. Rather than stay and drown, they should flee to higher ground.

Rather than perish in an impossible battle, they should retreat and live to fight another day. Counselors who instill common sense like this and a modest amount of self-esteem do good work and lessen many troubles. That is enough to justify their existence. They need not also be great philosophers, though people like me will always wish that they were.

CLERGY

If ordinary counselors present themselves as prepared to share our emotional upsets, clergy present themselves as prepared to share our struggles to discern the overall meaning of our lives. That is what we instinctively expect of rabbis, ministers, and priests. Sometimes they meet our expectations, being able to talk both modestly and deeply about God, evil, and the construction of ultimate meaning. Other times they do not because, strangely enough, explicitly religious issues embarrass them. They have come to define their role as facilitating an ethnic identity, or stimulating helpful social ties, or promoting programs to help the poor, unwed mothers, the homeless, any people struggling on the margins. Stark questions about death and pain, prayer and the nature of God, can make them blanch.

Therefore, as much as with secular counselors,

you ought to look before you leap into the counsel of a clergyman or clergywoman. What does he or she actually believe? What is the standpoint from which he or she will be listening to your troubles, taking stock, offering advice? Some clergy are excellent counselors, others are mediocre to poor. Counseling still figures as part of their general job definition, but not all clergy are comfortable with it or good at showing how faith bears on personal troubles.

In recent years what is often called "spiritual direction" has come on the scene to offer precisely religious counsel. Such direction assumes that sharing the ups and downs of one's efforts to grow closer to God, more comfortable and intimate with the ultimate mysteries, can generate considerable help. The director presumably has learning and experience in this area. The person seeking counsel pledges implicitly to bare his or her soul and take the director's counsel to heart. Good spiritual direction is a species of religious friendship, though by itself it tends to lack the mutuality that friendship implies. Generally, the director does not bare his or her soul to the directee, except inasmuch as that might illuminate the directee's concerns. Occasionally the director will have crisp and specific advice. More frequently the sessions will amount to a support of the directee's venture into the wilderness of God—assurance from one who has been there that the venture is beneficial.

Clergy who know their business are both modest about saying how divinity works and resolutely convinced that those workings are crucial. If they have lost their faith in the significance of "God," "grace," "prayer," and the other principal words that religious people are forced to use, they should get out of the business. Social work is a decent occupation, well able to stand on its own legs. It does not need a clerical collar or the mantle of a rabbi. A member of the clergy who does not pray, is not himself or herself putting faith to the test, is a menace. On the other hand, a member of the clergy who sees no connection between faith and social justice is equally problematic. Judaism and Christianity are religions of both/and. Their God is both the Creator of the world and independent of the world. In their traditional view, religion is concerned with both the here-and-now and the transcendent, the eternal, the hereafter.

The clergy are teachers and role models as much as counselors. They have signed up to pass on a tradition, keep alive a fund of wisdom about how the world hangs together and what human beings need to do if they are to prosper. Doctrine and morality figure prominently in the traditional concerns of the clergy. Their charge is to remind us how our religious community has construed the world and what it has considered decent, helpful, healthy, holy behavior. Clergy have to make their own peace with the politics of their particular religious denomination. Until they do, they are not likely to settle the doubts of their given congregation. A balanced view of the authority of the Talmud, or of the regional synod, or of the local bishop is usually enough. Either blind acceptance of religious authority or skeptical rejection usually causes difficulties.

Last, and relatedly, it is worth noting that when we go to a member of the clergy for counsel, we have the right to more than a private opinion, let alone the idiosyncratic views of a dissident, a heretic. Our rabbi, minister, or priest ought to represent and translate the long-standing tradition. It is the centuries of Jewish or Christian wisdom that give resonance to religious counsel. It is the long train of rabbis, divines, and monks who have petitioned God, endured great suffering, pored over every nook and cranny of both speculative and practical faith that is precious. When we find ourselves in deep trouble, we want no callow half faith, no latest fad. We want what has been tested and found solid. We want what the best and the brightest have made of God's inevitable darkness and our inevitable pain.

TEACHERS

The teachers who have impressed us are usually those who seemed bright, competent, clear, and caring. Slouching in with our books, we appreciated a little humor, signs of understanding. Then we became intrigued by the teacher's subject matter. He or she was able to bring math or history or biology alive. For the hour algebra or the Civil War or the endocrine system seemed important, intriguing, something well worth studying. We realized that our minds were made to stretch and grow in search of understanding. We realized that the past can illuminate the present, and that knowledge brings a kind of power.

This suggests that an impressive teacher knows, more or less explicitly, something central about the human vocation. We possess brains and time in order to become lifelong learners. Unless we keep exploring our world, ourselves, the mysteries right and left, we default on the promise we showed in the cradle, greatly shortchanging ourselves.

One of the central troubles that human beings fear is the waste of their potential. Again and again the sadness that people long to share with their friends or counselors is a sense that they're going nowhere. Too seldom does our public education convince us that we can always be going somewhere. If we defined ourselves as lifelong learners, we could be. There are always more intriguing places to see, more good books to read, more beautiful works of art upon which to gaze or to which to give ear than we have the time, money, or energy to enjoy. Equally, there are always further things to learn about ourselves, lessons buried in our past that still elude us. If we have been educated well, we need never lack for adventure. If we have been educated well, we are always indebted to a few good teachers —people who showed us in the flesh or through their books how becoming human is in good part a matter of continual schooling.

When we fall into trouble, we may of course search out revered teachers and request their counsel. We may also think about what such teachers implied we can do. Minimally, they implied that we can think about our troubles. As I elaborated in Chapter One, when describing how our minds work, what they always offer us, we are not helpless animals, condemned to run in circles. We can stop in the middle of the street, realize that our minds offer us distance, perspective, a kind of mastery over our troubles, and so escape the helter-skelter of our fears.

Simply by standing up to teach us, to share knowledge and tradition, teachers assert that it is good for us to think. Indeed, the more old-fashioned and rigorous the teacher, the more likely he or she is to demand that we think accurately, with discipline, after mastering the basic facts. Few gifts are more precious than what John Henry Newman called "the habit of philosophy." This is a training in rigorous, critical thinking. It is a disposition to put data together, force them to make sense, keep asking how they connect to other parts of our worldview.

Yes, the sad fact is that much higher education today downplays the possibility of a worldview, a sense of the whole, because a great many professors are narrow specialists lacking the habit of philosophy. But, to quote Eric Voegelin again, "Human beings will not live by depravity alone." Disease in the professorate does not mean that our minds are no longer healthy, that our souls no longer long for order, connection, a comprehensive and long view. We can't be human without this longing. As long as we live, we have to hope that our lives make sense.

The help that good teachers represent is the reminder, with or without concrete applications, that much of our trouble is always ignorance. We didn't know our own hungers, so we made a mess of sex or drugs or money management. We wasted our time in school, so we have no marketable job skills. On the other hand, it is never too late to start learning. Simply by reviewing the pattern of our two failed marriages, or the pattern of our drug-taking, or the way we've handled credit cards in the past, we can learn most of what we need to do better. Simply by getting some vocational counseling and taking ourselves back to school we can usually improve our job prospects.

DOCTORS

Just as teachers loom as good people with whom to share our troubles, because they should reinforce our ability to put our minds to our problems, so physicians can attract us. When they are experienced, made wise by their dealings with pain, their ability to heal can touch our spirits as well as our bodies. If we have started to lose hope, this spiritual healing can make all the difference.

In fact, both ordinary counselors and doctors usually realize that no trouble is either purely physical or purely emotional. Cancer would not be "cancer" without the fear it raises. The physical aspects of addiction, like the poor nutrition that poverty often brings, are significant factors in many troubles. We cannot think well if we are ravenously hungry or racked with cramps. Equally, we cannot think well if we are racked with grief. Always we are rational animals, embodied spirits, a fusion of matter and thought. Thus the great Danish philosopher Søren Kierkegaard satirized the claims of G. W. F. Hegel to have created a system that expressed the movements of the divine Spirit by noting how odd it was that the system stopped when the system maker had to turn aside to sneeze.

I have always envied doctors their regular involvement with people brought into crisis, though in more judicious moments I've realized that this probably puts doctors under great strain. Crisis sharpens our wits, releases our adrenaline, makes us think we are dealing with things of great moment and so are living significant lives. I assume that only a few years of actual medical experience demythologize this romantic view considerably. Still, more than once I've wished that I had not kept ruining my dogfish and so been forced to conclude that I didn't have the hands for medicine. More than once I've longed for the concrete satisfaction of being able to set a broken leg, or sew up a gashed arm, or prescribe a wonder drug to right a malfunctioning heart, even a malfunctioning personality.

People who can do these things for us rightly win our gratitude. When they have a good bedside manner, projecting patience, understanding, and kindness, we easily blow them up into heroes, paragons of talent and wisdom. Then they can seem natural sources of good counsel—if only they weren't so busy! Sometimes in fact they are sources of good counsel, so it is worth maneuvering through their busyness.

The image of *healing* our troubles interests me greatly, because many of the spiritual leaders who most influenced world history did much of their work under the rubric of healing. For tribal peoples, typically the most powerful figure has been the shaman, who is preeminently a healer, as well as the main repository of traditional lore. The Buddha refused to engage in speculative debate and described his teaching as practical, a kind of healing. It was not necessary to know all the ins and outs of nirvana, the state beyond pain and suffering. It was only crucial to break with ignorance and experience nirvana. To get lost in questions about the nature of nirvana was to be like a man struck with a poisoned arrow who insisted on knowing who had shot the arrow, what his lineage had been, what kind of bow he used, how far away he had been. Obviously, the crucial point was to get the arrow out and find an antidote to the poison. Obviously, the teaching that the Buddha proposed was not speculative but medicinal— healing for spiritual sickness.

Jesus also came on the scene as a healer. According to the Gospels he cured the blind, the lame, lepers. He raised Lazarus from the dead. The demons feared him because he cured the deranged they possessed. Like the Buddha and most shamans, Jesus did not distinguish sharply between the bodily and the spiritual. The first condition to be fulfilled, if he was to be able to cure people, was that they give him their trust. If they did not believe in his person and mission, he could do little for them. Moreover, it is legitimate to see Jesus' concern for the poor, his proclamation that a new social order was coming, as a broader sort of healing. Only the inrush of God could remove the deep malignancy, the radical social injustice, causing so much misery. Only when people repented and believed in the good news of the Kingdom of God could salvation—the Latin word *salus* means "health"—take hold.

So when you are minded to take your troubles to your revered physician, think of the healing you're after. Similarly, try out the model, the imagery, of healing when you seek good counsel of your friends, or your minister, or your therapist. Are you willing to make the changes in lifestyle that the restoration of health may require? Will you take the medicine, stay with the exercise, stay on the diet? Analogously, will you work on your habits of thought, which may well have become unhealthy? Are you committed to some tough reflection, the reform of your laziness, letting go of old excuses and neuroses? Until you are, what healers can do for you is limited. The conditions remain as Jesus laid them down: You've got to repent (be willing to turn your spirit around) and trust in the regime your healer lays out for you.

AUTHORS

I have entered "authors" as a category of people with whom it can be useful to share your troubles because my own deepest healing has come from meditating on classical texts. Some of these texts have been biblical. Others have handed on wisdom from Buddhism, Taoism, Talmudic Judaism, and Islam. I have read with profit books by many mystics. Good novelists and poets have also left me in their debt. Moreover, the simple act of reading quietly, slowly, ruminatively, has nearly always proved helpful, consoling. Whenever an author takes me to deeper waters, exercises my better spirit, I come away renewed.

Thinking about this, I have concluded that one of the many ways in which our current American population has been shortchanged, or has insisted on remaining uneducated, is in its reading habits. First, few Americans are regular readers of anything serious—perhaps 5 percent, booksellers estimate wanly. Second, fewer still know how to read contemplatively—so as to nourish their spirits, which work below their acquisitive minds. Usually people read for information: facts, figures, happenings, ideas. Or they read for escape—stories, more or less trashy. This leaves untapped the great potential of literature (writing both good and significant) to instruct and heal our inmost selves.

If you want to test this potential, put aside your models of speed-reading, and also your expectation to be passive. Prepare yourself to stop whenever something strikes you—to pay attention to the impact upon your spirit. Two sorts of impact are significant. A story from the autobiography of Ignatius of Loyola, the sixteenth-century founder of the Jesuits, illustrates them. Ignatius had been injured in battle. While he was recuperating, he ransacked the library in the castle where he was staying. It was longest on romances and lives of the saints. He read both, and after a while he realized they had curiously different effects on him. He picked up the romances with enthusiasm, and he loved to picture himself performing the great exploits of love and valor they described. When he put them down, though, he felt dissatisfied, even sad: They were unrealistic and had done nothing to nourish his deeper spirit. They had only provided distraction.

In contrast, Ignatius picked up the lives of the saints reluctantly, because he feared they would be heavy going and might challenge his worldly way of life. Once into them, though, he found a beguiling satisfaction. They were describing things of great moment: what was really important in life, how a holy person, a truly good person, would live. Eventually he decided he had to test for himself the claims that the lives of the saints were making. He set himself to try to become a saint. Thus leisurely, reflective reading changed Ignatius's life.

It is not my aim to make you reject the world and take up the penances of a would-be saint. It is my aim to suggest that a great treasury, a great source of healing and enlightenment, lies ready to hand in good books. The people who have been most successful in overcoming the perennial troubles of life, who have been credited with the most helpful treatments of how we can become more fully human, are available for a pittance in any good bookstore or library. Certainly, if they come from long ago and far away, we may have to scramble to catch their drift and style. Plato and Augustine, Dante and Shakespeare, the Buddha and Lao-tzu, initially seem strange. They cannot be skimmed. With only a little familiarity, however, we start to realize they are mining gold.

In addition, there are present-day writers with much to teach us, much to say about troubles like ours. I have mentioned Robert Coles and Eric Voegelin, the former quite easy to read and the latter quite difficult. I could mention storytellers like Andre Dubus and Jane Smiley, probers of the mind like Oliver Sacks and Susan Baur. Henri Nouwen offers lovely, readable books rooted in the riches of traditional Christian spirituality. Elie Wiesel is now as much a mediator of the Hasidic Jewish tradition as he is the conscience of the Holocaust. Any friend who loves serious, wise books and is interested in alleviating your troubles can give you a dozen further suggestions. And as soon as you find a good book, one that meets your needs and touches your heart, you need only dip into its sources to start casting your net wider. For example, if Robert Coles proves useful, note that he depends on Erik Erikson and loves novelists like James Agee and Walker Percy. So give them a try, too. Give a try as well to the classics of your own religious tradition. If you are a Muslim or Jew, make sure you examine an up-to-date study of the Koran or the Talmud or the Bible. The same if you are a Christian: Both the New Testament and the Old Testament are dazzling, when you have a guide to bring out the fireworks.

Once again I underscore that significant reading, reading to nourish your soul, is leisurely and personal. You should stop when a line strikes you. You should mull it over, let your imagination play with it, ask about its further implications. Above all, you should probe why it has cheered you, or wounded your vanity, or challenged your conscience and made you feel guilty. You should let the author, the text, become an interlocutor, a partner to a conversation.

The text is asking questions of you, more or less explicitly. You need only put yourself in the position of someone being addressed to begin to hear them.

You should ask questions back—challenge the author's assumptions, see where his or her convictions seem to lead. It is very difficult to do this with films, TV, or videos. They move on, with little time for reflection. Books are always there, waiting patiently to be picked up again. You can read a little book in two hours or let it nourish you for two weeks.

If we find that a book is nourishing us, slaking a deep thirst or bandaging a sore part of our spirit, we are fools to rush through it. We owe it to ourselves to digest it completely, so that it can become part of ourselves. That is how we grow in the contemplative life, the life of our deeper selves. We grow by taking to heart, making part of our deeper selves, good images and ideas, beautiful thoughts and scenarios, wise estimates of life and programs for change—for becoming healthier, less troubled, more mature. That is what the best authors work in our souls.

CHILDREN

What should we do about sharing our troubles with the children in our lives? Should we try to shield them, or will it be best in the long run if we take them into our confidence?

I vote for taking them into our confidence. When my nephew and niece last came to visit, I was hobbling around with what was then being diagnosed and treated as arthritis. My nephew, aged six, was leery of me: How had I deteriorated so badly since the previous summer, when I had been a wonderful playmate, able to pitch to him all afternoon and then toss him around in the swimming pool? I noticed him hanging back, physically as well as emotionally, so I decided to engage him with my physical troubles. I could not bend over to put on my socks and shoes, so I made him a midget butler. He had to fit on my socks, brush up my loafers, and then shoehorn me into them. He didn't like doing this, but gradually he got used to it. As he worked, I joked about how decrepit I'd become, contrasting my state with the acrobatics he performed spontaneously from a six-year-old's excess of energy.

While Sean was visiting, we learned that my trouble was not arthritis but multiple myeloma. I left it to his mother to pass on the explanation of this strange term, but I told him that, one way or another, things would probably work out just fine. The day he left, he kept asking me how I was feeling. He had a card for me, full of good wishes and love, but his sister thought it would be bad form just to hand it over, so he left it in my bathroom, no doubt thinking that eventually I'd have to go there, and when I did, the moment would be private. In the months since I last saw him, we have spoken often by phone. Always he asks me how I am doing, in fact, demands a full report. It is touching to find a six-year-old as solicitous and serious as a graybeard of sixty. Clearly, he feels responsible for me. I think it began with my socks. In his little fingers he felt my sickness and my need for his help. By including him, I've risked his early exposure to deeper emotional pain, because it will be harder for him to lose me. On the other hand, we've grown much closer, and perhaps he'll live many years having known death fairly intimately, not fearing it as a terrible stranger.

My wife grew up in a family shaped by premature death. She was seven when her father died of congenital heart disease, nine when her second-oldest brother, the liveliest, died in the Battle of the Bulge. Her mother, struggling to raise the four remaining kids, took to making her little girl, the youngest by seven years, her confidante. Denise grew up privy to her mother's worries, hopes, stratagems, even prayers to the Blessed Mother. Her experience was that she rose up to meet this responsibility. Prematurely, precociously, she went to her mother's side and became a sounding board. The price she paid was a lifelong worry about death and difficulty living in the present. The gain was great intimacy with her mother and few illusions about the precariousness of all things human.

More times than not our children sense our troubles. They know us too well not to register our worries, fears, depressions. We flatter them when we explain how and why we are struggling. We should not ask them to shoulder our adult's burden. We should do our best not to quench their childish joy. But simply by living in proximity to them, we've brought worry into their childhood. Despite our best efforts, it can no longer be carefree. Every time my father would lose a job, a cloud would return to my horizon. From the time I came to reason, certainly after I was eight, I always knew our finances were perilous.

Similarly, I knew that our family was sick emotionally, though I had no concepts such as "dysfunctional" with which to name this knowledge. My parents talked openly enough for me to understand the overt problems: drinking, loss of jobs, disappointment. I wish they had been better at discussing the deeper problems: self-disgust, sense of lives ruined, bitter hopelessness. I think I could have understood most of what they might have told me. I think I would have been better for having been made a junior partner. We never managed to sit down and discuss our problems rationally, as a set of burdens we all had to share. We never polled ourselves to learn precisely how each of us was suffering —for instance, what my having ill-fitting, shabby clothes had to do with my reluctance to set out for school. My sister was too small then to be much of a partner, but only a few years later, when I had escaped to college, she had the same needs. She too never became a partner of my mother's troubles, one

given the tools to understand. The more we understand, the more we forgive. Thirty-five years later
my sister still has much to forgive.

Sometimes parents in particular or adults in
general have to forgive children—their boorishness,
their thoughtlessness, the riot of their undisciplined
energies. More frequently and profoundly, children
have to forgive their parents and the other adults
who have formed them a dozen significant failures,
even a few serious sins. In part, children have finally
to become adults, passing from unqualified blame to
blame tempered with mercy. As they see their mistakes with their own children, as they too come in
over par, they realize that such mistakes are well-nigh
inevitable. Fiercely as they vowed not to do to their
kids what their parents did to them, they find one
day that they are erring in either the same or the
opposite direction.

The sins of the fathers and mothers are visited
on each new generation. Our human tragedy, sym-
bolized in what Christian theologians call "original
sin," is that we are all born into an imperfect, tilted
situation. From the outset the atmosphere at home,
the surrounding political environment, the state of
the world, the state of the church or synagogue, is
tainted. The adults rearing us have significant shortcomings. Often—one wants to say usually—they
manage to offset them by loving us without qualifi-
cation—assuring us we can always go home. But

they are not saints, and we suffer from their sins. They are not models of wisdom, and we suffer from their follies. Unless we finally forgive them for being so human, we keep kicking against the goad uselessly. In the final analysis they chose us no more than we chose them. As in an arranged marriage, we've been bound together by others for better or worse. If we make sure that we spend our final days together reconciled, we shall overcome one of life's most grievous troubles. Like David lamenting for Absalom, the parent who dies unreconciled carries a most bitter grief beyond the reach of our healing.

GOD

The last one with whom we consider sharing our troubles, to whom we contemplate unburdening ourselves, is God, though if this book were an avowedly religious treatise, God would have to have come first. What do I mean by "God"? To our embarrassment, we students of the world religions find that the term is not simple or obvious, especially regarding Eastern traditions. In such "Western" traditions as Judaism, Christianity, and Islam, however, God is usually understood to be a personal absolute.

By "personal" I mean possessing intelligence and will—able to understand and decide. By "absolute" I mean free of any dependence on others—

independent, autonomous. For the Western theisms, God is the only absolute. Indeed, often their philosophers capitalize the term: Absolute. Everything depends on God and God depends on nothing outside him, or her, or it.

As personal, God can take initiative and establish relations with other beings, most notably other persons (centers of intelligence and will: traditionally, angels and human beings). As absolutely personal, however, God is not a "center," at least not insofar as that figure, that image, implies limitation. God possesses intelligence and will without limit, infinitely. We limited human beings cannot imagine or understand this concept, "infinity," adequately. We can only approach it by negation—by saying that God is not this and not that: not bound by a historical period, or a given culture, or one sex, or any physical barrier.

So, first, I understand "God" to be a personal absolute. Second, I want our discussion of God to retain overtones of the biblical deity that has shaped the theology, the understanding of divinity, working in the minds of most Jews, Christians, and Muslims. That is to say, I want "God" to be compatible with the Creator depicted in the first three chapters of Genesis; the Father to whom Jesus prayed; Jesus himself as incarnating divinity and suggesting its salvific activities (those that heal a fractured creation and humanity); and the sovereign Allah revealed through Muhammad and the Koran. For present purposes, these traditional overtones provide sufficient precision: God knows all, has all power, can understand our situations fully, can love us more intimately than we can love ourselves.

From this sketch of "God" it follows, first, that it is easy to share our troubles with God, because God already knows them. As soon as we accept a traditional Western description of God, we legitimate this conclusion. Thus, second, "sharing" with God requires us only to refer our troubles, our situation, our selves to God, using whatever images of him we find most congenial. In Chapter Five it will emerge that such a "referring" is a good, adequate description of praying. Here we may bracket the further connotations (for example, reverence, worship, and desire for forgiveness) that praying can carry, concentrating simply on opening our hearts to the full mysteriousness of our lives and creation—the God who is always present as the context, the ground, the whole in the midst of which we grope after survival and meaning.

Now, some religions hedge their bets concerning the goodness of God. However, none of the primary Western religions does. In Judaism, Christianity, and Islam it is axiomatic that God is light in whom there is no moral darkness at all—that God is sheer goodness, has no mixture of evil, no truck with wrongdoing. God is just in all his or her being and doing. God is always on the side of right, honesty, creativity, love, salvation.

Therefore, in referring our situation to God, we are sharing our troubles with One wholly positive. As Jesus put it, when we ask God for bread, we should believe we will not receive a stone. On the other hand, God is not a being as we are, not another creature, not limited to what our minds can work out, the range of "good" responses we can imagine. If we are going to share with God all the way, we have to give God a blank check. We cannot dictate how God is going to help us solve our problems. We cannot demand that God make us win the lottery, or overcome our addiction without struggle, or even retain our life against cancer.

Cutting across all the middle moves, we should see from the beginning that if our sharing with God is going to become a wholehearted petition for God's help, we have to let God work as God sees best—which may mean our seeming to get no good answer, receive no this-worldly victory. With a real God, not an idol of our own making, the bottom line of prayer should always be that his will be done, not ours. And even if we are not praying to God, are merely trying to connect our troubles with the divine mystery, we ought to realize that we are, by definition, getting in way over our heads. God is the prime mover. We are always running to catch up.

Of course, once we admit the primacy of the

divine mystery, we are already in way over our heads. Indeed, even our admission or nonadmission can seem irrelevant. Whether or not we think we believe in God, we live in the midst of mystery, never knowing clearly where we came from, why we are here, where we are going. Neither atheism nor orthodox theistic faith takes this mystery away. Fundamentalists who think faith absolves them from ever having to struggle for meaning are simpletons headed for a crack-up. Atheists who are sure there can be no meaning in their lives have no logical defense against suicide.

Granted all this, how do we best share our troubles with God? Very simply. We acknowledge the mysteriousness of our situation, treating all that we do not know as though it indicated the presence of an Other of a comprehensive order—a personal absolute responsible for creation, fully aware of the whole of history, both cosmic and human. We also treat this presence as though it cared about us, were wholly good and loving. Then we lay out our pains, our regrets, our sins, our hopes, our angers, the grievances we bear God, the tender shoots of the better self we'd like to nurture. If it helps, we review the story of our trouble, though God knows it in every detail. Then, having done such things, having exposed ourselves fully to the divine mystery, we stop, grow quiet, and listen.

At this point our sharing with God is somewhat

like the sharing with an author that I described. We are trying to create a dialogue. Just as we gave the author's text a life of its own, imagining its asking us questions and posing questions of our own in return, so we want a give and take with God. The difference is that we should remind ourselves that, though less specific than a book, God is also less subjective. Psychologists fear that "God" is usually a projection of our needs, entirely manipulable. People trying to give the divine mystery its due, to let God be the God that the Western religions have depicted when at their best, insist that God is prior to all human thought about him and utterly unmanipulable.

God is the regularity of nature, and also its apparent chaos. God is the unremovable darkness and silence at the edge of our minds, defining their expanse. When we feel collected and connected to the source of creativity, we experience a proper mysticism—a true feeling of union with God. But this is not our own doing. It comes and goes as God chooses. So the mystics, the people most authoritative about God's being and ways because they have most directly experienced them, insist that God is always prior, never manipulated. They also insist that they know little about God. God is always more unlike than like our best utterances about him.

What is the profit of sharing with God? It gets our troubles out of the closet, into the most comprehensive framework possible. As well, it puts us on the verge of asking the One responsible for the evolution that made us who we are, and that shaped the circumstances in which we live, to help us out, give us the strength—the trust, the courage, the deep-seated honesty—we need to do better.

At this point we have to sense that God is merciful as well as just. We have to find in "God" a source of new beginnings. God has to be eager to forgive us and help us to make a new start. God has to love us for what we are and what we want to be, putting aside the failures we feel we have been in the past. With God we can let ourselves face our worst fears, our greatest shame, our most bitter regrets, because even when our hearts condemn us, God is greater than our hearts. With God we can reach rock bottom, point alpha, the place beyond which there is no place to go. God is absolutely solid. The mystery is never going to go away. When we begin to realize that our spirits, our deep selves, find this primordial fact a constant source of nourishment and freedom, we have grasped the first principle of a spiritual life that cannot fail.

Bernard Lonergan, who wrote a marvelous book called *Insight: A Study of Human Understanding,* found that certain important insights are "inverse." By this he meant that sometimes what we understand is that there is nothing to understand. For example, evil is intrinsically irrational. By definition, it is doing what is not right, just, owed. Sin is irrational

—evil that we freely choose. To deal well with God and make the divine mystery the first principle of our spiritual life, we also require an inverse insight. The light must dawn so that we realize we are never going to understand God—that God is intrinsically, unavoidably, beyond us.

The divine mystery is not a collection of problems. As the mystics keep chanting, it is a light so bright that it blinds us, that we are bound to experience it as darkness. To become intimate with it, we have to "unknow" worldly knowledge. We have to give up our tendency to assault it as we would a problem, learning to wait patiently for it to reveal itself as an intimate, at times even shy and vulnerable, lover. All this is very strange, yet unfailingly invigorating. Take your troubles to God, pour out your soul to the divine mystery, wait attentively, and you will never lack for wonder. You will often, indeed regularly, find your perspective restored. You will gladly confess that, much more than you deserve, there comes over you an unearthly peace, at times even a taste of heavenly joy. I am no mystic, but even I can sign my name to this declaration. The mystery never fails to nourish and heal me. I know that my spirit has been made to contemplate it, to love it as the central reality and treasure of my being. It is my lever for moving the world.

CHAPTER FOUR

Deciding

OVERVIEW

ONCE WE HAVE THOUGHT WELL ABOUT OUR trouble, sifted through our feelings, and shared our findings with others, we face the matter of deciding what to do. The more fully we recognize what goes on in the process of deciding, and what good decisions require, the better we are likely to fare. Thus, I sketch a list of ingredients that go into a good decision. As in the previous chapters, my sketch is not exhaustive. However, by going through it thoughtfully, you should be able to equip yourself fairly well to make good decisions.

First, we reflect on the importance of *imagining concretely* what your decision entails —what it is leading you into. Here the work we have already done on imagining should prove helpful. If you discipline yourself to run through what the week of vacation in San Diego is likely to involve, you will be better equipped to decide whether you are up to it—whether going is prudent, wise, likely to turn out well. The same with a more harrowing decision such as walking away from your abusive spouse: Where will you go, how is he likely to react, what will you do with the children?

Second, as you decide, you have to *weigh the advice* you have received. Assuming that you have shared your troubles, you now have to assess what your sharing has yielded. Has the advice of family members, friends, counselors, and others been consistent, fallen into a steady pattern? Or has it been contradictory? The time has come to listen to your own best instincts, to hear what you yourself sense is best.

Third, there are methods for pinning down this process of hearing yourself, making it seem less obscure. You can lay out with pencil and paper the *pros and cons* you are finding. You can rule off two columns, one for pluses and one for minuses, and tally them up. You can even give numerical weights to such pluses and minuses—a heavy plus adds a ten, a light minus subtracts a four. By pushing yourself, stirring your imagination, you can objectify parts of your decision, which is much to the good.

Fourth, having collected the data for your decision, you do well to deal with your own attitudes, your emotional state. For example, you only help yourself by laying out on the table your *fears*. What is your worst nightmare in this decision? Do you wake up drenched with sweat because you have dreamed that your leaving has so infuriated your husband that he has tracked you down and beaten you to death? Have you worried that if you stopped getting blotto with whiskey each night, you would find yourself so hateful you couldn't bear it? Often we don't do what we should, can't make the decision that will spring us free, because we are afraid. When you can name your fears, you've got a hammerlock on a major enemy.

Fifth, are you willing to *entrust yourself to the future?* Have you got a sufficiently positive attitude toward what will be, toward "life," toward "God," to think that your tomorrows really could be better than your yesterdays? Until you do, you're likely to remain stuck in time present. We walk into a new scenario willingly only when we hope it will be better. Our hope should be realistic, and we can never expect guarantees, but we have to muster enough trust to get us over the hump—take us to new ground we cannot survey fully ahead of time.

Sixth, we do not make good decisions when we are *euphoric*. Good decisions require that our feet be on the ground. Thus masters of the spiritual life are uniform in counseling sobriety, prudence, discretion. If you are flying high, enjoy it but do not make a major change in your life. Wait until things have settled down, come back closer to your normal outlook. Don't marry in haste only to repent in leisure. Live with the guy for a while, actually or at a distance, before you hitch your wagon to his star. Make sure you know him, have seen all his moods.

Seventh, similarly, don't make important decisions when you are depressed, desolate. *Desolation* is no more trustworthy than euphoria. The best decisions come when we are sailing on even keel. We are most likely to choose well when we can say our choice matches up with what is reasonable as well as attractive and invigorating. When we are depressed, nothing seems possible. Hope thins out and our thoughts turn unduly negative. So when they are down, prudent people make no crucial moves, keep their money in the bank, wait for the sun to reappear.

Eighth, the state of soul from which good decisions spring finds us at *peace*. Our prudence and free will stand at level balance, like the pans of a sensitive, precise scale. We are able to read the data and our own moods accurately. We are what contemplatives call properly "indifferent": No undue passion pushes us ahead or holds us back. We can do what makes sense, seems right. No agenda from our unconscious is distorting our thinking, messing up our mind. With a full acknowledgment that we can always make a mistake, we can yet decide confidently, sure that we are doing what truly seems best, convinced that not to decide would be irresponsible.

Ninth and last, a good decision ends with a commitment to keep track of what *results*. We realize that making decisions is an ongoing process. Wisdom comes only through trial and error. Each evening we should review what we have decided in the course of the day, so that in the morning, when we plan the next day, we can avoid yesterday's errors. By getting burned, children learn not to put their hands on hot stoves. Children can be smarter than adults. All the books about smart women making dumb choices about men must come from some actual case histories. Why does x or y never learn? Usually because they will not discipline themselves to reflection. Facing the results of their choices is too painful. By the end of this chapter, you should know better.

IMAGINING CONCRETELY

When I came home from the hospital after treatment for my broken back and the insertion of a two-foot rod in my diseased right femur, I received an invitation to preside at a wedding in San Diego.

The date was two months away. Though I seldom perform such services, the invitation came from the son of old and close friends, so I wanted to oblige him. Thus I gave a tentative yes, marking off the dates on the calendar. *If* I had recovered sufficiently, I would gladly travel to be with them. In fact, Denise and I began to plan a little vacation by the sea.

As the deadline for the decision, I set a date two weeks before we would have to fly off. By bad luck that time found me in the pangs of withdrawal from powerful chemical medication. As I imagined myself trying to negotiate through airports, what it would be like hobbling to the beach, how I would manage the horrible aching in my bones apart from the helps of home, going to San Diego loomed as possibly visiting hell. I hoped that once my body adjusted to the withdrawal, I would feel better, but on the day of decision I had no guarantee.

So I punted. I knew that my friends were prepared for the contingency that I would have to say no. I had already helped the young couple clarify what they wanted for their ceremony, and I sent them a polished version of the talk I had planned to give informally. With some regret, but no substantial judgment that I was making a mistake, I postponed my return to normal activity until I was sure I had recovered more fully. Indeed, I asked myself whether I had not been foolish to expect that two months would be sufficient to recover from the heavy-duty trauma I had gone through.

The example, of course, is only illustrative. The point to stress is the value of imagining as concretely as one can what effects taking a proposed step, making a suggested decision, is likely to produce. As long as I thought vaguely, generally, about being with our friends, sharing in the wedding, relaxing at the beach, maybe riding around the superb San Diego Zoo again, the trip seemed a fine idea. I had to get down to cases, such as my needing a wheelchair in each airport, the hassles of driving on the San Diego freeways, how little walking I would actually be able to do on the beach, before I had a realistic scenario. I had to remember all the pills I would have to bring along, the walker and cane, the fatigue visitors now brought me, the strain of adjusting to a different diet, bed, regime for exercise, struggle for time to read and pray.

Imagined with a certain ruthless objectivity that allowed for worst-case scenarios (friends were getting stranded in airports, travel was up 5 to 10 percent), the vacation trip seemed imprudent. There was no critical need for us to go. We were responding to no emergency. Better to let go of a little dream we had worked up than risk getting ourselves into a painful situation. I would have come home to a fresh round of chemotherapy. That was no time to be exhausted. When we totaled the pros and cons, the sum was a solid negative. Our friends understood completely. We settled the matter with them in peace. Afterward we had mild regrets, because I rebounded well from the withdrawal, but the major objections remained. All in all, it was a good decision. Most likely, there would be other chances to see our friends and vacation by the sea.

Imagination is not reality. What we foresee is never what actually occurs. But foresight, predictive or anticipative picturing, is a powerful tool for making good decisions. On the basis of past experience, we can project what is *likely* to happen. If old Sam has been a bore nine out of the past ten evenings spent together, tomorrow night is likely to be a snoozer. If Sally hasn't been able to make up her mind the last three times you've gone shopping with her, you'd better plan on a long stint in the boutique tomorrow.

The same with your preparation for an exam, or your pattern of handling alcohol, or your probable response to a surly child. The same for your visit to the unemployment office tomorrow, or next week's dinner with your bearish in-laws. We have to leave space for surprises, but surprises are not the best rule of thumb. The best rule of thumb is that the past is the most reliable guide to the future. While staying flexible, we are foolish not to plan ahead on the basis of experience.

Finally, note that the more precisely you imagine the details of the venture about which you are deciding, the sharper your preview is likely to be. You can do better than merely picturing the dinner with the bearish in-laws globally, as an undifferentiated lump. You can remember the questions regularly raised about the children's schooling, your participation in abortion rallies, even your choice of clothes. Let the slow burn they have created in the past return in imagination to singe your chops now. Get yourself ready, lest you explode once more. Indeed, consider giving yourself a break: Maybe it's time to develop a migraine. Maybe this is a dinner invitation you should postpone.

FACTORING IN ADVICE

A woman finds herself unhappy in her second marriage. Though the man seemed a fine match, thoughtful and stimulating, after a year he seems to have lost interest. He is mildly affectionate, but no passionate lover. He likes to have her around, but she doesn't feel taken seriously. He listens to her stories from work, offers helpful advice, but has no comparable place for her in his work life. Significantly older than she, he often seems to treat her as a younger sister or even a daughter, seldom as a full partner. This is not the intense, romantic, captivating adventure she sought. This is frustrating, depressing, even boring.

Already feeling guilty because she failed at her first marriage, the woman panics at the thought of a second divorce. Two smudges on her record are more than she can bear contemplating. She believes in marriage and frowns on divorce, though hardly legalistically. She has taken to heart many of the precepts of the women's movement, but she is no radical. And she worries about the effects of the deteriorating situation on her children. The girl was never enthusiastic about this remarriage. Now she is turning surly. The boy seems bewildered by his stepfather, largely because the man makes so little effort to treat him as a son.

The woman is stereotypically feminine in keeping active a solid network of friends. Each week she makes sure she stays in touch with half-a-dozen other women. They share what they are going through, lamenting over lunch or the phone. They give and take, coming to know one another's psyches well. So now the woman draws on their knowledge of the first year of her marriage to help her get in focus what she is starting to consider a crisis. Two of her friends have never been impressed by this husband, never found him suitable for her. Perhaps predictably, their feedback is sobering: She should start to face the possibility that this marriage will never work out. The other four think she should go slowly, treat herself to a lot more patience, downplay the negative reactions of the kids (who are bound still to be adjusting), and try to talk things out with her husband, even get him to go with her for marriage counseling.

The woman suspects the man will not be enthusiastic about marriage counseling. She feels in her bones that he is not unhappy with the marriage. He likes having her around. Some of the conversation is stimulating. He continues to bury himself in his work as he did before the marriage. He seems to feel no great need for more than occasional sex. And he writes off the gripes of the kids as normal adolescent unattractiveness.

Thus the woman thinks her husband unlikely to make any significant changes unless tied to a stick of dynamite. Patience is fine. Talking things out would be better. But something keeps itching in the back sectors of her mind. Something tells her this marital trouble runs deep. She dreads the intuition, but there it is. What should she do about it?

One thing she should do is compare her information and analysis with that of her friends. What does she know that she has not told them, perhaps could not tell them? What prejudices does she find in their outlooks, when she makes herself think critically? Joan has kept her first marriage together for eighteen years, but only by making significant sacrifices. The woman therefore has to wonder whether this friend can be objective about a possible need to call things quits. On the other hand, Pam, the most vocal of the two urging a hard look at pulling out, is down on men at the moment. Only a month ago she broke, painfully, with her housemate of four years. It's hard to think that her advice isn't marred by much pain. Most crucially, though, the woman has never told her friends about the increasing awkward-ness of sexual relations with her husband. She is not the type to pass on bedroom tales. So her friends do not know how rejected she feels, how starved for affection. She's lost a lot of self-confidence, and she wonders how long it will be before she's wounded dangerously.

We can leave the further chapters of this story to the woman's own honesty. In my intuition, unless she can get her husband to face what his lack of interest and affection is doing to her, she's going to walk away from him. As I imagine her character, she's too strong, too feisty, too much in need of emotional and physical intimacy to put up with a loveless marriage. At some point not too far down the road from where we leave her, she's going to decide that her survival requires pulling out.

On the way to that point, though, she is wise to reflect on the advice others have given her. People who know her well and have her best interests at heart have given no consistent feedback. She has found no ground swell either for staying or preparing to leave. Certainly, she finds well taken the point of the majority that she should be patient and do nothing hasty. She agrees that she must try to get her husband to talk, ideally to seek counseling with her. But her own judgment, emerging ever more clearly, is that her pain is more than mild discontent. When she faces it head-on, she sees that it runs deep. She is angry, disappointed, and feels cheated. She is not getting what she signed up for, what she thought she was promised. Even judging herself rigorously, she has to say that she has been generous with her husband. She has gone at least 60 percent of the way. As long as he feels there is no problem, she guesses she'll remain at least 20 percent distanced—significantly short of the intimacy she craves. With a chill she intuits that she has already made much of her decision.

PROS AND CONS

Since childhood I've been intrigued by arithmetic. Even today I play games as I swim my laps: eight done, seventy-two make a mile, therefore eight ninths to go; twenty-nine done, seven short of one half. On occasion I've wondered how to quantify the factors of a decision. For example, would it be useful to offer young professors, as a *rough* rule of thumb, the expectation that they publish a scholarly book every five years, or publish two scholarly articles each year? I've never been tempted to think that such a quantification could substitute for qualitative judgments never fully articulable, but I have thought that we are remiss not to avail ourselves of the clarity that numbers offer us.

Thus I tend to think it a good exercise to sub-ject a decision to an analysis of pros and cons that tries to weigh them. For example, once we had to decide whether to move from one city to another to accept a new job. The interview for the new job had gone well, the potentially new school had made us an offer, but we were content in our then-present setup. Driving home, we discussed the pros and cons. The more exactly we specified them, the clearer the more advantageous choice became. For example, the new salary was not simply better, it was 40 percent better. The benefits were not merely more generous, they were 50 percent more gener-ous. The students were more gifted, by an average four points on the ACT scale. We could not pin down so precisely the likely stimulus of our new colleagues, or the better feel we had about the place of our discipline in the new school's design for the humanities, but maybe "a third more appealing" came close to what we were feeling.

As I listened to the mounting enthusiasm in Denise's voice, I ran through the cons on my list. We were comfortable in our present situation—but maybe in danger of moldering? We had wonderful friends, and no guarantee we would find their like in the new city. Perhaps most poignantly, we had lived less than two years in a lovely new passive solar home we had designed just for our particular lifestyle. How would we ever replace it? How heavily ought giving it up to weigh?

Eventually we decided that we should not stay put for a house. The gains we could anticipate in moving were both practical (financial security) and idealistic (better conditions for our work). The losses might be things we could replace or minimize—by making new friends, staying in touch with old friends, rousing some imagination to assure good new living quarters. By the time we had finished the half day's drive home, the decision was two-thirds made. We'd need a few days to comb through it, making sure there were no major snarls. We'd have to see how giving up the new house and leaving good friends sat in our psyches, and how realistic the hopes for better work in the new situation looked in the clear light of morning. But our minds, hearts, wills, had shifted. To our surprise we were less rooted in our old situation than we had thought. A new challenge had moved us fairly easily. By setting down the pros and cons rather precisely, we helped ourselves see the apparent rationality in moving. Seven years later we have no regrets.

That was not a traumatic decision. In many

ways we could not lose. As I write, another decision is looming, one more daunting and dangerous. When ordinary chemotherapy fails to arrest multiple myeloma, one can go to megadoses. That ups the ante, but not discontinuously. It's still the same game. However, when the megadoses fail, the last option is to transplant bone marrow. That changes the rules and stakes considerably. That's a decision harrowing even to ponder.

A bone-marrow transplant is an effort to effect a truly radical cure. The procedure kills the patient, as far as blood and marrow are concerned. The existent marrow is rendered dead by X ray and radiation. Unless other marrow, either taken from the patient previously or donated by a compatible outsider, takes hold and produces a new, healthy blood-and-bone system, the patient never recovers. Even with the best screening, such failure occurs 30–40 percent of the time with multiple myeloma. Statistics on other aspects of the outcome are fragmentary, because the procedure remains quite new. Already, though, it's clear that remissions can be merely partial: Survival does not guarantee the return of full vigor. It's also clear that the short-term effects of the procedure can take the patient through the far reaches of hell: extreme nausea, diarrhea, fatigue, headache, blistering; depression, hallucinations, mental breakdown. All in all, a bone-marrow transplant is not something to be undertaken lightly. Even the financial factor is staggering: perhaps $250,000 (not covered by much medical insurance★).

Reading about bone-marrow transplants, I found my pace slowing. I did not want to know these things. Much in my mind and will was resisting. Still, I had to begin to face this bottom line. At what point would it be better to kiss my life goodbye, knowing it had been richly blessed? What obligations did I have to fight on, even if the last battle loomed as the harrowing of hell? Was I worth $250,000? Would I make any future contribution to justify so much fuss? And suppose I emerged as one of the partial survivors. Would I be content to limp along another dozen years, one of T. S. Eliot's half people, "living and partly living"?

I have listed the pros and cons mentally. In brave moments I have weighed the physical pains lightly, telling myself I might be able to bear a few weeks of misery. Thus far the telling factor has been the tears in my wife's eyes. If I could spare her some years of loneliness, all the risks might be justified. If she wanted me to try, I'd probably have my decision made. Of course, how could she want me to try, or not to try? My possible suffering would appall her, yet she'd want me resurrected to health more than anything else in the world. So eventually I'll have to

---

★ New developments, such as using only chemotherapy and employing more outpatient facilities, may cut costs significantly.

settle the matter privately, in the wilderness of conscience where either yes or no reveals an abyss.

FACING FEAR

I am afraid of a bone-marrow transplant.
Slowly, the fear is lessening, but my first reaction was
to recoil totally. I thought I could handle the solitude (because the immune system is destroyed—no
white blood cells—the patient must spend weeks in
isolation). The physical reactions were horrifying,
but I've learned a little about enduring pain. What
most frightened me was the possible assault on my
mind and spirit. As one doctor put it, as quoted in
Paul Wilke's book *In Mysterious Ways: The Life and
Death of a Parish Priest* (an account of the progress of
a patient with multiple myeloma through a bone-
marrow transplant), we simply cannot imagine ahead
of time the emotional or spiritual impact of so radical a biological assault as this kind of transplant.
There is no way of predicting what toll the procedure will exact on the mind and will—on the basic
personality. Typically, patients who survive emerge
significantly changed. They have traveled to a place
few others have had to visit. Even their doctors can't
understand fully what they've gone through.

The little marine in me thinks this procedure

might be the ultimate challenge, but the mature man in me tells the marine to shut up. There is a fear that mature people know is healthy. There is a hubris, a dangerous pride, that brings disastrous miscalculations. What are my tools for facing the fears inherent in this future? How should I start to talk to myself about such an eventuality? You catch me here in midstream, not certain of my journey, but perhaps my report is the better for that.

First, I have postponed any decision about the transplant, concentrating on present business, which is ordinary chemotherapy and rehabilitation. Sufficient for the day is the evil thereof. Certainly, I am bound to find the question of a bone-marrow transplant percolating in my subconscious. Now and then a daydream reminds me it's alive and well. But I have consciously decided not to let myself get lost in imagining what might have to come to pass. It does no good at the present to picture constant vomiting or mental breakdown.

Second, I am trying to stay free, radically indifferent to both life and death. This, obviously, is a tall order. But I have lived more than fifty years (the life span of most people less than two centuries ago). By the actuarial tables I would probably die within twenty-five years even if healthy. I would not want to languish in decay during my last years. I'd want full mental vigor, which no one can guarantee. So dying well, with a certain peace, painlessness, and dignity, is not a bad scenario. Indeed, it is a valid option to set alongside a bone-marrow transplant. I'm not sure I'd be justified in electing it, but I shouldn't feel compelled to take extraordinary means to preserve my physical life.

Third, what do I think about dying, afterlife, immortality? I think it is all a great mystery, the supreme unknown. My religious faith says that God wants to take us into the divine deathlessness. "Eternal life" is the capital phrase, taken from the Johannine writings of the New Testament. No one knows what "eternal life" means. The images from Revelation are a dazzling but questionable translation.

If there is a God, and if God is love, then eternal life is the creativity, light, warmth, and complete fulfillment we sometimes glimpse in love. If death takes us from this present, often painful, existence into such a completely fulfilling love, who could not count it a blessing? That is the way saints of many religious traditions speak. That is how many mystics seem to transform their sufferings. I'm not sure I want to live at their extremity, let alone if I am able. I only know it is good for death to seem pregnant, mysterious, not necessarily the worst of evils. I only know that setting a procedure such as a bone-marrow transplant in the bigger perspective of ultimate meaning, possibly eternal life, makes contemplating it more bearable.

TRUSTING THE FUTURE

To avoid paralysis in decision making (the five-dollar word is "abulia"), we have to trust the future. Unless we believe that decisive action can improve a situation, we have no strong motive for taking it. Naturally, trusting the future involves trusting ourselves—believing that we can engineer change successfully. However, it also involves making peace with reality as a whole—with what I have sometimes called the divine mystery. Stay close now as I muse about this peacemaking in terms of letting go of worry.

A few years ago, when I had no thought of cancer, I was meandering through John of the Cross's *The Ascent of Mount Carmel* when I came across a remarkable passage. The saint dismissed worry with disdain: Worry never does any good. All worry is vain. By temperament I am not a worrier, but I know several people who are. So I wondered how John could be so categorical. What allowed him to blow away so human a reaction to our frailty?

I decided it was his personal experience. *The Ascent of Mount Carmel* describes what people who want to be fully free can do to liberate themselves. Complementary to it is John's *Dark Night of the Soul,* which describes what the divine mystery does—how

God acts in the depths of such a person's spirit. Together, the two actions, human and divine, take away all this-worldly security, leaving the person nothing finite, created, to lean upon. No material possessions, or doctrinaire thoughts, or warm-fuzzy emotions remain untouched. All are lost in a wilderness, a darkness, in which the human spirit can see nothing, must move by blind faith.

Eventually, this milieu can become congenial. With time the human spirit can come to love the darkness, because it alone offers full security, at times even full satisfaction. The darkness is not going to desert us. If we bet on not-knowing, we can never go wrong. Moreover, we can begin to live simply, wholly, from the heart instead of the head. By love we can go where our minds are helpless. When free of all dependence on things less than the divine mystery, we can find the world rid of all threats.

This is an experience, a vision, a goal far beyond my comprehension. But if it removes worry and opens up the future, I'm all for pondering it. Suppose we face the possibility that our worry is finally useless. Suppose we digest the old chestnut that we cannot add a cubit to our height. The best of diets and lifestyles cannot guarantee us twenty more years of heartbeats, full protection against cancer or AIDS. At some point we have to make our peace with a perilous world. Sooner rather than later, we are wise to say, "What will be will be." Our first recitation of this mantra may be naive, spoken with a fatuous though probably unreflective assumption that "misfortune will never slash me." Still, a second naïveté is possible. Even slashed, we can realize that the future remains open, that precisely how our cancer or AIDS or alcoholism will end is not clear. So, childlike and unworried, we can let come to be what will.

Perhaps a smaller example will help. Take a university in which individual departments have long been assigned inadequate operating budgets. Let the head of such a department realize two things. One, other heads ignore these budgets and regularly overrun them without penalty. Two, it does no good to play ball honestly with superiors, because they take away any savings one has garnered by being frugal. Has the time come to "sin bravely," as Martin Luther used to urge? Should one cast aside the Puritan conscience and join the overrunners, not from wantonness but because that is the rational thing to do? A major hurdle to doing so may be giving up the temptation to worry. The system has fed on underlings' having a stricter sense of accountability than their superiors'. It has penalized responsibility and rewarded laissez-faire. So to hell with it. Let those responsible for the irrationality of the system do the worrying. Theirs is the shame, the sin. Let them bear it.

One can imagine parallel decisions, snatches of

freedom, in families that finally hold Dad or Junior responsible for his follies. No longer will Mom or Sis wring her hands and keep cleaning up his messes. What will be will be, and Dad or Junior will be responsible for it. Assuming that the matter is relatively minor, if he gets hurt, the pain will also probably be minor. But maybe it will wake him up. Maybe the iodine will sting him into changing his ways. That would benefit everyone.

Naturally, we worry when we sense danger of significant damage, someone getting hurt seriously. But even this worry can be useless. If we have been prudent, thoughtful, and so done what we reasonably can, we have to let other people exercise their freedom. Many things fall outside our control. We can do damage as well as good by trying to play God. We have to trust that the future will treat all parties fairly. We cannot worry as though the game were so tilted that we should not play it lustily, sinning bravely.

EUPHORIA

Contemplatives, closely attuned to the movements of the inner spirit, have long studied variations in their moods. Earlier I noted the example of Ignatius Loyola, who learned volumes about himself while reading his way to recuperation from war injuries. All masters remark on how an intense spiritual life tends to bring times of euphoria. One feels inspired, renewed, washed free of all problems, wonderfully energized. God is in his heaven and all is right with the world. What ought we to think of such a delicious experience? How ought we to make it bear on significant decisions?

We ought to think that this is a splendid gift, with much to teach anyone about the best of human potential. However, we also ought to think that euphoria is nearly bound to prove passing. Therefore, it is no mood in which to make crucial decisions. It is no valid indication of how we are likely to feel 75 percent of the time in the future. Our hormones will sink. The planets will go out of phase. We have no guarantee that the Spirit of God will continue to move us so palpably.

For good decisions we need a realistic assessment of what we can bear, what we can expect of ourselves, day after day. If you get along well with Charley only when he's wining and dining you, you'd better not marry him. If you're not a morning person, you'd better not sign up for the five A.M. class on meditation. Conversions seldom change basic personality structures overnight. In most cases it takes years before we eradicate old vices and install shiny virtues.

Western spiritual masters have sometimes called euphoria "consolation." In the intensity of their experiences, tears of joy have played a large part. They have wept to find the world so beautiful. They have cried that God has been so good to them. Joy has moved them to transports of praise. In some cases these dispositions seem to have remained relatively stable over many years, though most such masters also report periods of intense "desolation"—loss of joy, apparent abandonment by God. Their regular interpretation of the alternation of consolation and desolation is that they are learning the nature of ultimate reality.

In itself, ultimate reality is perfection—what the Hindus call "being-bliss-awareness." As we engage with it, however, this perfection comes and goes. We cannot sustain a pure perception of it. It does not yield itself up once and for all. Especially, we need to learn that it does not exist for our exploitation. It is what it is whether we are enjoying it or not. It is no less real when we cannot feel its beauty or goodness or love than when we can. For our own sakes, we have to learn this painful lesson. We will never be wise, realistic about our limitations, until we come to love the divine mystery for its own sake, not for what it does for us.

Few of us have to worry about ruining our eyes by weeping constantly from joy at the divine beauty. Most of our euphorias are much smaller gauged. Still, we do have to worry about clearheadedness. We are wise to make our decisions in times of emotional peace. Good friends will remind us of this truism. We should also tell ourselves to enjoy the current high but not plan on its staying. Indeed, it is staple contemplative advice to expect to lose one's euphoria, and also to expect that desolation will pass. Most people go through ups and downs, highs and lows, almost cyclically. With time the mature learn to discount both the peaks and the valleys. Most crucial and revealing is what we do in ordinary times. If, as Freud wanted, we can love and work steadily day by day, we are in good mental health—likely to make good decisions and avoid lots of trouble.

DESOLATION

The downside of our emotional lives is desolation. Most of us get depressed, at least now and then. Most of us have days when we feel jittery, out of sorts, graceless. Occasionally we can point to specific causes for this negativity. We drank too much, or we got very tired, or we overexercised. Usually, though, we have to write it off as a fallow time in our biorhythms, a semiregular hour of darkness on our biological clock. The main point regarding decision making is that this hour of darkness is no time to make changes. We should no more trust what we think or feel when depressed than what we experience in times of euphoria.

This is not to say that we cannot learn from our desolations. They show us what rock bottom looks like. For religious people they suggest the core sinfulness afflicting human nature—how out of sorts we are without divine grace. So we are wise to take away a dose of humility. Desolation is profitable when it helps us see ourselves as sensual, fragmented, people who need help to carry on. Desolation should never make us despairing. The hope that cannot fail lies outside ourselves, in the regularity of the divine mystery. But for the moment the divine mystery seems inattentive, or even condemnatory. We cannot believe that any outsider, including God, could think well of us, because we cannot think well of ourselves. So our pain is sore isolation. We see how unattractive we are on our own.

Desolation calls us to a blinder faith, a deeper trust, than what we need on good days. It reminds us that how we feel is not the best index of how we are doing. How we feel is in good part a matter of animal health. If we are vigorous, we are likely to feel good, capable, ready for action. If we are sick, or tired, or sore in back or brain, we are likely to feel miserable, and so to think ourselves miserable beings. It may be that we are no different in virtue than we were two days ago, when everything went swimmingly. A migraine is no proof that we have fallen out of favor, become wretched morally. A migraine therefore becomes the occasion to abandon ourselves to the divine mystery. "Here I am," we can say, "help me out."

The greatest mystics and saints usually speak of profound desolations. They came to know how little they could do by themselves. The cracks in being that split every creature became very familiar. They saw that there is little health in human beings when they close in on themselves. Unless we remain open to the wider vistas of the mystery, we seem narrow and unattractive. But remaining open in this way is not fully within our power. Thus we depend on what we call good fortune, or good biorhythms, or the grace of God to be broadly gauged and attractive. We depend on something or someone outside, other than ourselves, to be what we are at our best.

People prone to depression have a terrible foe to battle. Few things are harder than getting up day after day when one's head is heavy, weariness is a constant companion. If our prospects seem dismal, we are heroic simply to keep going. Many people would not show up for work were they not responsible for spouse or children. Creative, fulfilling work is not guaranteed in our culture, and probably it is much rarer in many other cultures.

I believe it helps mightily to confront one's depressions in prayer. I believe that forcing oneself to come to grips with ultimate questions—for example, what in fact we can reasonably expect from life, or from other people, or from our work—takes away much of the overhead. The task on any given day is simply to endure to the end with integrity. Accomplishing more than that is unnecessary, gravy. The first rule of the spiritual life, as of the biological life, is survival. Sufficient for each day is the evil thereof.

People who have been in heavy trouble know this instinctively. Not for them high-flown ideals of immaculate performances, perfect 10s. They are grateful to crawl into bed at night with their skin intact. They give glory to God if they can say they have preserved their consciences. On better days higher ideals will return to charge them. When grace or good hormones flow abundantly, they will perk up their ambitions. But the wisest among them will always refrain from making important decisions during depressions. The wisest will seek help merely to keep plodding, keep fanning a little flame of hope that before long things will change for the better.

PEACE OF SOUL

Modern Americans don't know what to make of the "soul." It is an old-fashioned term, gone the way of Plato and Aristotle. Here I mean nothing technical by it. It merely names the rock-bottom self, the inmost "holder" of our being and identity. More important in this section is "peace," which I have already described as the tranquillity of order. A good decision flows from a moment, a mood, a disposition of peace. We act best when our soul is collected, integrated, making a whole. When our soul is fragmented, or shaded by emotions such as envy or greed, we are likely to act unwisely, toward our own hurt and the wounding of others.

Say that you have gone through the pros and cons of a significant decision. The new job offer clearly is desirable, or the second husband just has to be left. Also, you have checked your own emotional dispositions: No fear is shaping you unduly, you have a healthy hope for the future, neither euphoria nor depression has warped your judgment. At this point the thing for which to look is a telltale peace in the depths of your being. When you go to the bottom of yourself, you ought to find a supportive simplicity. No longer are arguments running back and forth. No longer are waves of emotion tossing you up and down. Your essential being is at rest. In patience you are possessing your spirit.

This is not a state of soul you can manufacture at the snap of your fingers. When it lasts for several days, it reflects a hard-won decision. You have brought yourself to a new orientation. Looking away from the old job, you have set your face for the new. Closing the door on your old husband, you are looking down the walk for something fresh. And your mood is upbeat. You are not giddy, but you feel that your times are in joint. It is good for you to be moving on. For everything there is a season, and just now you are in the right one. You know that this peace is vulnerable. Yet for the moment you cannot doubt it—it is strong. Not to act out of its fullness would be to deny what your self is saying. You would stagnate, and so sicken.

We may call the experience of peace of soul a moment of grace. For a change, you are moving smoothly, hitting each measure of your music. Normally a bit awkward, held back by bad habits or pushed forward by untoward needs, you find being graceful novel. Yet you know that this style is right, how you ought to be regularly. Just as animals move instinctively, with no thought of how to stalk or pounce, so you ought to be more instinctive, spontaneous, harmonious both inside and out. A good decision expresses a moment of grace and sets us up for more such moments in the future. It stems from a time of health and facilitates further healing.

In the Bible, both the Book of Genesis and the Epistle to the Hebrews exploit the notion of a Sabbath, a regular time of rest. A good decision, flowing up from peace of soul, is restful, sabbatical. A bad decision is restless, restive, flowing up from a soul still unsettled. The reflective, contemplative pauses necessary to inculcate peace of soul, therefore, tell us much about our human vocation. If we are to live gracefully, with the animal fluidity we ought, we must rest regularly. Unless we withdraw, center down, settle to the bedrock of our being, we won't hear the music of the spheres, let alone move along with it easily. Peace of soul is not a luxury. It is essential for fully human, healthy, happy living. What you learn in the privileged moments of good decisions bears rich implications for your reform, the improvement of your whole future lifestyle, the sabbaticals you should take regularly.

FOLLOWING RESULTS

You have put your good decision, marinated in peace, on the table. Well prepared, it has tasted sweet and proved nourishing in the outcome. The last part of your business as a student of good decision making, a person who wants to know how to get out of trouble in the future or, better still, avoid trouble completely, is to school yourself to take stock of the results of your decisions. If you go over the results of your decisions regularly, checking what happened to your original estimates of what doing *a* rather than *b* would bring, you can continue to learn important things about yourself, about the process of making decisions, and about the objective world in which you must operate. Naturally, you can never pin down any of these things once and for all, but you can become sufficiently aware of usual patterns to make more and more good decisions, fewer and fewer bad decisions.

To formalize this discipline of checking the results of your decisions, I suggest reviewing your day each evening. As you lie in bed, tired but often still lucid, give yourself a few minutes to replay the main events of the past sixteen hours. What did you set out to do in the morning, over your Wheaties? How realistic does your planning now seem? What did you overlook or fail to take into account? Why did your boss's anger surprise you? And what about your own emotions? How did they vary from morning to evening? Did you find again that midafternoon sent you scraping the bottom? Is that simply a matter of low blood sugar? Ought you to take a walk, a catnap, a strong cup of coffee, time out for the self-help of a pep talk?

This review, which many contemplative traditions might label a nightly examination of conscience, should proceed gently. It does no good, and much harm, to beat yourself up for your failures. Virtually no human day passes without fumbles, outbursts of temper, moments when we are dumb or vain or distracted. To err is human. To forgive ourselves is to stir our hope that the divine mystery is merciful. A major benefit of a regular review is that it offers a steady stream of new beginnings.

We can bury the old day spiritually as well as

physically. Just as sleep is a figure of death, so can making amends at midnight be. We can hand ourselves over to the night that holds our meaning. We can let the darkness, the inscrutability of where we stand in the cosmic scheme of things, have the properly last say. Reconciled to not knowing always, yet cheered that we have made our try, we can let go of our squirming and turning, asking humbly to sleep the sleep of the just.

The accounts we settle by examining our conscience regularly tell us most of what we ought to bring to good counselors or spiritual directors. The states of soul we find night by night tell us how it goes with our pursuit of peace. If we are reviewing our days rightly, the line of trouble in our soul will dip steadily. Even before we have tidied up our affairs practically, we can settle most things emotionally. As it becomes less and less fearsome to visit our depths, face our selves, we can experience forgiveness. It is not so terrible to realize that much in us is a screwup. That judgment can now stand as a simple truth, a merely objective reality.

We have black hair, brown eyes, and a tendency to make a mess of money. On the past record, and from what we still see lurking in our instincts, we respond to the wrong kind of man, or woman, or business opportunity. Nine times out of ten partying with Kit leaves us in a stupor. Why, then, don't we stay out of Kit's way? Because much in us remains

dumb and weak. Can we accept this factual judgment without giving in to it? Where is the happy
line between taking ourselves as we are and agreeing
to remain underachievers?

Each of us has to learn whether our conscience
tends to be too strict or too lax. If you do not know,
and you are a beginner, start by assuming you are too
lax. Hold yourself to an exact accounting, and see
what happens to your behavior. When you find that
you are becoming tight, neurotic, overly anxious,
worst of all scrupulous, you can ease off. Because it is
hard to get an objective judgment all on your own,
you might discuss this matter with an outsider you
trust.

A scruple is a pebble. The original image calls
up something that gets into your shoe and raises a
welt, makes you sore, soon threatens an infection.
Clearly, then, a scruple is an enemy of your peace of
soul, and so something you must cast out speedily.
Sensitive people often go through hellish trials because of scruples, but a firm outside authority should
make it clear that scruples finally are narcissistic—just
another form of the self-centeredness that is the great
stumbling block in the spiritual life.

Scrupulous people refuse to trust the divine
mystery. When their hearts issue a condemnation,
they cannot hear the Johannine assurance that God is
greater than their hearts. We can never find ourselves
just, holy, fully in the right. Any review at midnight

is bound to find us imperfect, sinful debtors. Once and for all, we have to trust that there is grace to save us. Remembering the times when something we could never have planned on swept in to carry us, we must let go of the sum of all our decisions, all our efforts fine or shabby, and let ourselves believe that all shall be well.

CHAPTER FIVE

Praying

OVERVIEW

OUR LAST MAJOR CONSIDERATION DEALS WITH various ways of engaging the comprehensive mystery of our existence, the global context of our troubles. To gain peace of soul, and so significant leverage against the deepest threats of our troubles, nothing is more helpful than reconciling oneself to the way things are under God's stars.

First, we examine this matter by discussing what I call *secular prayer*. Many people who never darken the door of a church, synagogue, or mosque try to reconcile themselves to cosmic reality, make their peace with the way things are. I find some of these people more admirable than professedly religious people, more honest and loving. Consequently, I am drawn to sketch for them a praying they might find fully authentic. To launch it, they need only confess that they are not the center of the world.

Second, we examine explicitly *religious prayer,* which for our purposes will be theistic—oriented toward the personal God featured in the Western religions. This prayer centers in worship: pure praise of the holy mystery. However, it allows, even encourages petition: asking God for the things one needs. It is interpersonal, ideally a friendship or even love affair between the self and its deity. It can mature to the mighty proportions of the famous mistranslated line from *Job:* "Though he slay me, yet will I trust him."

Third, we take up *meditation,* the kind of "prayer" most favored in Eastern religions. Certainly, devotional branches of Hinduism and Buddhism urge personal approaches to gods such as Krishna, Buddhas such as Amitabha. Nonetheless, the basic spiritual discipline taught in most ashrams and monasteries is an emptying of the mind that pays devotional deities little heed: meditation. For example, this is the central discipline in Zen, whether one is "just-sitting" or boring into a koan.

Fourth, we discuss religious *contemplation:* the holistic recollection that pushes love to the fore and makes thought secondary. Whereas a purely intellectual contemplation, such as the *theoria* pursued by classical Greek philosophy, found the act of thinking divinizing, the Western theistic religions have found love the more godlike action. Thus Christian monks East and West, devotionally minded rabbis such as the Baal Shem Tov, and Muslim mystics such as Rumi and Rabia have all panted for love, even found love to be the gist of their dark nights, clouds of unknowing, lamentable stretches of loneliness.

Fifth, we deal with *petition*. What may we ask of the divine mystery? Does it make sense to beg help in our trials? What warrants do we have for doing this? How fitting does the image of Abraham haggling with God to spare Sodom now strike us? All of us are simply people. Our lives are short. None of us has ever seen God. In our frailty, perhaps we have a claim on the divine majesty. Or is this kind of thinking demeaning? Ought we to hold back from asking for help, to maintain a proper dignity?

Sixth, how can we know if our petitions are *answered*? Are the files from miracle shrines such as Lourdes clear proof? Miracles are tricky business. Thaumaturges like Jesus, who presumably knew his stuff, only work "signs" carefully, if not indeed reluctantly. Human nature is often credulous. The line between faith and superstition can be slim. So it is well to be highly critical of claims to dramatic answers from God, miracles in a strong sense of the term. Usually the answers we receive take the form of new dispositions. Circumstances may have improved only slightly, but our state of mind can become markedly new.

Seventh, eighth, and ninth, we deal with three fundamental spiritual virtues spotlighted by praying: *faith, hope,* and *love.* Though they have become staple in Western theism, one can trace them back to pre-Socratic philosophers such as Heraclitus, who argued that they are requisite for all spiritual health.

Faith is the ability to go beyond facts and entrust oneself to life positively. It is not opposed to reason. Indeed, it expects reality to reveal itself to be intelligible. However, faith must oppose rationalism. The strictly logical mind can account for only part of what we need to know. This part is important, nothing to be despised, but it cannot do the whole job of making us happy or wise. We learn crucial things about nature, ourselves, other people, and the divine mystery only by trusting them, indeed by loving them. Love creates the most arresting kind of knowledge, that which arises when the other drops all defenses and stands before us naked.

Hope moves beyond faith to lean into the future. Hope is not optimistic, not facile. Sometimes it must take the form of "hoping against hope." Then its grounds stand revealed as nothing human, nothing created. Its grounds are only the divine mystery, which is never defeated, which can always make all things new. Thus Israel has kept hoping for its Messiah. Christianity still awaits Christ's return. And Islam anticipates the Judgment Day of Allah. Collectively, these spiritual hopes mean that more than two billion people the world over are stretching their souls toward the future, living expectantly. God is their absolute future, a horizon of unlimited possibilities. Therefore, nothing need ever dead-end them.

And, of course, God is their love. The divine mystery is their consuming passion. If the 80 percent of the American people who say they believe in God know what their answer implies, four out of five of our fellow citizens may be passionate for God, at least now and then. Four out of five may on occasion pray erotically, to a mystery beautiful as well as much needed.

The love to which praying conduces is a hunger for light and life. Whenever we respond to something or someone beautiful, to something or someone vulnerable, to an act of bravery, courage, signal honesty, creativity—to anything positive, noble, good—our love of the divine mystery takes wing. What attracts us comes from this mystery and educes it. There is no significant beauty that does not take us out of ourselves, take us into a "more" that seems sacred.

Relatedly, whenever we hate evil, ugliness, injustice, cruelty—all that mocks creativity and what is right—we also love the divine mystery, send up petitions for God. So the love at the heart of praying is nothing less than our naked humanity: what we would go toward and what repels us. The more human we are, the more love defines us, feeds us, tells us our destiny. Praying shows us that this love has no restrictions. Engaging with the divine mystery, we can never say "thus far and no farther." Our reach continues to exceed our grasp. Praying shows us both where "heaven" comes from and what "heaven" is for.

SECULAR PRAYER

I have wonderful friends who go to church or synagogue, but I know of crooked preachers, smarmy bishops, rabbis with egos that reek. So I cannot confine admirable humanity to religious people, nor keep unreligious, secular people cordoned off from the divine mystery. In my book admirable humanity arises where people pay attention, are intelligent, show themselves reasonable, act responsibly, and, above all, comport themselves lovingly. The divine mystery shines in each of these rises of consciousness. Whenever one finds a person truly honest and loving, one finds a person intimately involved with God. Whether or not that person feels "religious" is secondary.

Secular prayer, it follows, is simply the dealings

that people who do not consider themselves religious, who define their province as this-worldly matters of space and time, have with the divine mystery. Unless they are dim, such people are well aware that their lives float on a fullness they do not understand, will never get their minds around. They make no claim to be the center of the world. Thus a first-line scientist such as Albert Einstein urged us to look at what scientists do, not what they say. What he himself did as a physicist convinced him that so-called "scientific materialism" was a bankrupt philosophy. A scientist without a spiritual life was a miserable human being, perhaps even a contradiction in terms.

The same with apparently secular poets and businesspeople. We should regard what they do more than what they say. If their spirits go out in transport to beauty, they know about more than space and time. If they keep their integrity despite immorality all around them, they know about a conscience unjustifiable on worldly terms. There is no unspiritual, unmysterious human condition. There are no living people beyond the power of nature, or a child, or a beautiful lover, or a righteous cause to shake up their soul and change their life. The monsters of moral depravity who seem closed to all decency force us to be cautious, but by actual counting, they must be less than 1 percent of our kind.

So the vast majority of human beings are candidates for praying, regardless of how they describe their sense of ultimate reality. How so? Because they take pleasure in the cloudless night, when the stars seem to hang only a few yards above them. Bedding down in the Tetons, they let themselves exhale in awe. Or, like Whittaker Chambers absorbed with the whorls of his little child's ear, they confess that children, flowers, even designs of a cell stagger their imagination. Annie Dillard, the pilgrim at Tinker Creek, read out some of the numbers, the staggering profligacy, of the critters living along a simple stream. Instinctively, she followed Whittaker Chambers, many naturalists, most of the rest of us dazzled from time to time, and gave vent to a natural reverence, even a protoreligious awe. Kant had his starry heavens above and moral law within. Those of us who have been loved freely, gratuitously, beyond all our merits, carry a powerful reason for prayer.

Secular prayer could be merely the sustenance of natural awe, the prolonging of a natural wonder, veneration, sense of gratitude. Simply let your spirit grow quiet, as it asks you to do, and linger with the mystery in which you feel placed. Enjoy the sparkle new in her eyes. Ride the intake of breath it causes. But notice also the enlargement of your spirit. Falling in love is mystery's best thing.

People who pray, whether secularly or religiously, risk falling in love with the world, creation, reality. No matter how much hardship they must reckon with, they keep having the experience of grace. Reality has something radically unowed about it, something that need never have been. That it is, and that we have it, is more than we can fathom. The move of the healthy spirit is to be thankful for it, despite all the pains it can cause. The praiseworthy motion, as we know without having to think, is to be happy to be here—grateful to have been invited to enter in. In fine, the right word to respond is small and simple: yes. Affirmation is the nub, the sufficient beginning, of a salvific prayer. When we can say yes to our lives, without blinking away any of their troubles, we have grown into our maturity. When we do say yes to them, we are at the business of prayer, risking a great transformation.

RELIGIOUS PRAYER

I take religious prayer to be an intercourse with the divine mystery that treats it personally, as a force both intelligent and decisive. The God of the Western traditions is the Creator of the world who made it freely and purposefully. The biblical God is also a redeemer, one bent on "buying back" people constantly inclined to sell themselves into moral slavery. The Christian God chose to incarnate the divine Word, live among us as a full human being, suffer, die, and be resurrected—all to inaugurate an era of unlimited hope, an aeon in which all people may become partakers of the divine nature and so possessors of eternal life. These are huge claims, large mouthfuls. Nonetheless, we can understand the actual prayer of Western religious people only if we admit such claims as the backdrop of what actually goes on in most mosques, synagogues, churches, moments of private devotion.

Your prayer is religious when to the divine mystery you submit yourself as the pot, not the potter—as the creature, not the independent, autonomous maker of your own being and time. From this beginning there echoes a primal acknowledgment: I have not made myself; I am someone else's more than my own. This is a curious acknowledgment, both unsettling and soothing. On the one hand, if I am not the captain of my own vessel, how can I sail authoritatively? On the other hand, if I am the captain, how vulnerable is my voyage! On the one hand, I want to take charge of my life, make my way freely, create a handsome self. On the other hand, with only a little experience and honest reflection, I realize that I am ignorant, weak, limited in a hundred ways. Apparently, I shall always be, for I see no other human beings wholly different. Perhaps, then, it is only honesty to admit that I need another's keeping, or that another's keeping can beckon attractively. Perhaps in seeking religious security I not only want to regain the intimacy of the womb but also to affirm the radical truth of my being: I do not explain or fulfill myself.

Suppose that I find this radical truth nourishing, a source of order for my soul. Suppose that watering the depths of my spirit, where mere facts and figures bring no growth, brings me more of my self. Is it not right, legitimate, even imperative for me to do this? Am I not obeying an elementary law? When confession is good for the soul, it makes the soul humble. Neither the starry heavens above nor the moral law within are my doing. Neither falls under my dominion, changes at my behest. So I should submit to these more original, powerful realities, not expect them to submit to me. I should dispose myself to worship: praise of what is obviously greater.

The power of nature, ripping through the sky in a storm, is more than I can fathom. The miracle of birth, how the cells have made a new human being, ought to hush all my babbling. Something awesome is asking for my awe. The color purple is demanding a royal response. I should give it. When I do give it, I am praying religiously. When I name the mystery my Master, what Islam calls the "Lord of the Worlds," I am bowing low in spirit, just as a creature should.

The history of the world's religions is structured by this bowing. Mircea Eliade, a pioneer in researching such history, saw experiences of sacredness everywhere. Everywhere—in every historical period, on every continent—men and women have sometimes felt struck by or drawn into something more than ordinary. Now and then a reality realer than their human own has imposed itself, demanding recognition. Instinctively, all premodern peoples tried to order their lives in terms of this realer reality —in terms of their intuitions of sacredness. What they had felt in privileged moments of revelation furnished the models for how they wanted to live. Their work, sex, eating, warring, hunting, and farming all floated free, risked senselessness, unless fitted to the cycles of nature in which the sacred so regularly expressed itself. Their myths, rituals, songs, dances, convictions about death, and hopes for rebirth all expressed an intoxication. They were drunk with the brew of the sacred. The mystery had blown them away.

We cannot become premodern people. Our natural world can never be mysterious as was theirs. But we live in the same universe. We die just as painfully. Now and then joy also surprises us. Now and then we too hunger ravenously for a real, stable, unfailing reality. Religious prayer allows any of us to express all this passion, need, emotion, ricocheting thought. Bowing low to what is beyond us, we can let our spirits rip.

We need neither appear for prayer nor leave with a fistful of answers. We don't have to show that we've always been good. We need only open our hearts, pour out our souls, howl, lament, shout forth our amazement. We need only be deep with the mystery, full, showing it all that we've ever wanted. We need only shake our fists, open our arms, both attack and let ourselves be ravished.

MEDITATION

Contrapuntal to this Western passion is the sober decorum of Eastern meditation. In practice such decorum can vanish when the crises of enlightenment draw near, but in the beginning Eastern meditation approaches as a cool breeze, a most rational exercise. All life is suffering. The cause of suffering is desire. If we stop desire, we stop suffering. Meditation is the primary way to stop desire. What could be more cogent? How lovely the Buddha's refutation of our disorder. Only the dull would not be charmed. Only the rabid would say he could not help us.

The first verses of the *Dhammapada,* a much-loved Buddhist text, sum up the rationale for meditation: All that we are comes from how we think. If we think, speak, are filled with evil thoughts, pain follows us as the wheel follows the ox that drags the wagon. If we think, speak, are filled with good thoughts, happiness follows us like a shadow that never leaves.

The crucial reality is mental. Meditation bets that by changing consciousness we can change our world, ourselves, our fortune. We cannot remove evil physically. Despite our progress in the natural sciences, we still cannot prevent flood, fire, or famine. Today, as 2,500 years ago when the Buddha was preaching, suffering flourishes all around us. Indeed, all life remains laden with pain. All human beings still have to die. Most sicken, lose much they love, fear old age, loneliness, failure. To be human is to be vulnerable. To live even a year is to feel risk. Life is intrinsically perilous. Simply feeling this, recognizing this, causes suffering.

But there is a way out. Sitting under the bodhi tree, the Buddha capped his apprenticeship to the gurus of his time by breaking through to enlightenment. In a flash he saw that suffering holds us only through desire. If we want nothing, we can break free. When life is no special treasure, death loses its sting. When sickness is no worse than health, leprosy doesn't matter. There is a space within us we can master. There is a sovereignty we can claim. We need only conquer our desire. When the flame of our burning goes out, *nirvana,* existence that is not mottled by suffering, swings into place.

The Buddhist program for putting out the flame of desire and sending people across the ocean of suffering to nirvana has three principal parts. We must act properly—be moral. We must understand properly—be wise. We must meditate—transform consciousness. These parts reinforce one another. We should act in view of wisdom (the way things are) and from the peace of a clarified, collected consciousness. We will understand rightly only in function of a right behavior and meditational practice. And we will meditate well only if we take traditional wisdom to heart and are divided by no strong vices. All for one and one for all. The three parts of the program are like legs of a tripod.

The meditation urged by the foremost Buddhist masters is far more intense than the laid-back versions one finds in most new-age groups. At its most brilliant, Buddhist meditation is nothing less than a full-scale assault on the ordinary (what biblically based Western masters instinctively call the "worldly") mind. That mind dichotomizes, breaking reality into "this" and "that." It speaks of a distinct self standing apart from the cosmos. It is alienated from the primary wholeness of reality-in-itself. It thinks and feels in terms of defects, failures, deficiencies, whereas enlightened people know that reality itself is perfect.

In a word, the ordinary mind is ignorant. (Why so is not clear.) Meditation is the practical way to overcome this ignorance. Experientially, with a force no one can argue away, it can tip the ordinary mind over, break it free from its ignorance. In a dazzle of light, with a flood of joy and fulfillment, the person victorious in meditation realizes what the Buddhas have all proclaimed. Beyond what words can indicate, the victor gestures or smiles as though reborn, verifying the verses from the *Dhammapada*. We are indeed what we think. Our world can indeed become beautiful, complete, perfect. Nirvana is the inmost reality of everything. By nature our minds are wholly clean. Because meditation can remake us to this conviction, we owe it serious consideration.

CONTEMPLATION

It is not hard to learn about meditation, Eastern or Western. Most cities of one hundred thousand or more have Buddhist or Hindu meditation groups. Most also have Christian monasteries. Either will usually furnish a start. To learn about contemplation, the monasteries are the best bet.

Here "contemplation" signifies a Western prayer, clearest in the history of Christian spirituality, that makes love the central focus, without denigrating the mind. In positive form, such contemplation often fixes on images. Eastern Orthodox Christian spirituality, which is deeply concerned with icons, offers a good example. In both its public liturgy and private prayer, the Orthodox tradition tries to fill the senses with good hints about God. Thus pictures of Jesus, the Blessed Virgin, and the saints dominate Greek and Russian churches. Incense and melodious chant wrap themselves around the worshiper sensually. Convinced that divinity has come into our midst and taken flesh, the Orthodox tradition of contemplation believes that we can find traces of God everywhere. The world is not so fallen that beauty is bound to mislead us. Our own flesh is not so corrupt that it is not a trustworthy image of God. And, above all, the rapt contemplation of Jesus and the saints can take us to communion with our deity. We need only open our eyes and ears, only let our perception take in the living summary of Christian faith available in the icons, and we can participate in mysteries of salvation.

Western Christian spirituality has developed equivalents of this positive, iconic contemplation, as one can find, for example, in *The Spiritual Exercises* of Ignatius Loyola. There the person following Ignatius's lead goes through a series of meditations and visualizations focused on the Christ depicted in the gospels. However, Western Christian spirituality has also developed a strongly "negative" contemplative tradition. One can find equivalents in the East, but such Western masters as John of the Cross and the anonymous author of *The Cloud of Unknowing* have perhaps made negative contemplation the mainstream of Western mysticism.

This negative contemplation differs little from what I have already described several times when speaking of the divine mystery. The basic fact that we dwell in the midst of a reality we cannot understand has been my fulcrum in this book. If we would get to the roots of our troubles, we must come to terms with our radical ignorance. We shall never master life as though it were a mathematical problem. We shall always need to cast ourselves upon its waters, as pilgrims living by faith. The leading masters of the spiritual life simply sharpen, deepen, and clarify this universal necessity. Their great merit is to show us why we always depend on the mystery and how we may come to love our constant dependence.

What I have loved in negative contemplation is the relief it offers. My mind clatters along, hour after hour. Entering into the cloud of unknowing finally stops my mind. I need no longer pay attention to all its images, questions, snappy sayings. I can take on ballast and move down to the bottom of my self. What is going on at the top becomes secondary, almost unimportant. That I am, not independently but by the grace of the mystery, steps forth as the primary wonder. When I simply abide in this wonder, calling it the creative love of God, I feel warm and fed in spirit. I have found my place in the scheme of things. I sense no further questions. There is nowhere else I need to travel. Momentarily, I live at the omega and the alpha, the end that is the beginning.

Necessarily, any talk about these matters is paradoxical. One is trying to square circles, frame voids. So talk tends to vanish. The clever, upper mind, realizing it is babbling, lets the heart take over the play. Abiding connected to the mystery, the heart simply loves it. Shabby or polished, the heart can just be what it is. "Heart speaks to heart," the venerable saying has it. Hunger, affection, need, desire, regret, hope—all pour out as variants of heartfelt love.

None of this outpouring need be souped up emotionally. All can be either ardent or calm. Being is more significant than doing. The night is dark, one needs only to stay still. The night is also nuptial. John of the Cross was a great fan of the Song of Songs. The exchanges between the soul and the divine mystery play out a commitment that is covenantal—the wedding of heaven to earth. God is present as God has promised to be: in the midst of our lives, at the center of our beings. We will not find God apart from our trekking. Any transports from time soon return us to our bodies, our stories, our people's common history. Still, contemplation proves that we are not just our bodies. Our stories stand revealed as tales of spirit. History itself points beyond space and time, because space and time alone furnish history no consummation.

I cannot urge you to negative contemplation unreservedly. If the darkness holds no appeal, negative contemplation is not for you. Until you're sick of thinking and feeling, the dark night is bound to repel you. Until you sense that healing is a work of unpredictable love, you're not up for this kind of wedding. I do not say this to be elitist. There are many other ways out of trouble, most of them simpler, safer, easier, perhaps on the whole better. I say this matter-of-factly, sensing that at this point I'm largely alone. Most of my audience has probably departed. The film is running down to the last credits. It is my peculiarity that I love these credits above all others. It is only in my story that these last need be first. So you need only taste and see whether negativity bears you the goodness of the mystery. If it does not, go easily in peace. Love the other ways you find the divine mystery alluring. Fortunately, God's provisions for handling trouble are legion. In our holder's house there are many mansions.

PETITION

To many people the first connotation of "prayer" is asking favors. Indeed, an earlier English put this into common speech: "Pray thee, may I have an apple?" "I pray thee, hold me excused." We are nearly bound to ask favors of the mystery. We come to it wholly needy, so how else should we speak? Who among us is not hurting, feeling incomplete or dirtied or misused? Who among us does not carry burdens in conscience, sins we need to scrub off? None of us can be sure of the morrow. All of us have debts, fears, pains, regrets, hopes so vulnerable we fear to keep on carrying them, lest they break our very hearts. Our children, jobs, bodies, houses, friends, projects can all seem terribly fragile. Our parents, spouses, and perhaps above all our selves can all seem frail reeds. We need help wherever we can get it. A wonderful place would be someone or something not needy, someone or something rich enough to give help away.

This someone or something is the mystery, or God, or the benevolent Buddha. This is what lies beyond us while being our source. This is where the world originally came from. This is where the world must end up, if it is not to burn out. Grant the existence of a divine mystery, take a fullness of being and significance to heart, and immediately you've set up a petitionary situation. What is more natural, more obvious, than to ask one's source for help? To whom else should we go, if all others are like us, partial and intrinsically limited? Prayer of petition is neither unusual nor strange. It is virtually a law of our being, as much to be expected as breathing or eating.

However, there is asking and asking. To beg help to make it through the day, handle one's troubles, is normal, right, proper, perhaps even obligatory. To beg to hit the lotto, or to avoid paying one's taxes, or to escape responsibility for one's children is to put oneself in the wrong. The mystery is not a substitute for taking up your rightful burdens. No praiseworthy prayer helps you remain immature. The parts of handling our troubles that we can manage never leave the kitchen table. Always they stay there, demanding our attention. We may need help from what seems beyond us to control our alcoholism. Even if we get it, though, we'll have to avoid Joe's Bar and Grill. The divine mystery will not teach us keyboarding. The local junior college is the place for that. So we should not ask God for what we can do ourselves—what we know we should do ourselves. We may ask God to help us do what we know we should do, but this prayer only spotlights our weakness. It does not sanction a desire to cop out.

Second, when we ask things, helps, of the divine mystery, exposing our manifold need, we should align ourselves to God's will. We cannot know God's will, except through the suggestions of traditions we consider revealed and authoritative (for example, the Ten Commandments). God's will is part of the divine mystery, and so it never becomes patent, obvious, something we can pick up and stuff in our back pocket. We never grasp the full sweep of creation, how all the myriad parts of the puzzle fit together. So in simple modesty, the mere truth of our limitation, we ought to pray provisionally: as you wish, as you find good. This, in turn, creates a mood that all theists say pleases God. It shows a winning trust. Who is better able to take care of us, secure our well-being—God or ourselves? If God is good, as we assume when asking God's help, shouldn't we hand ourselves over to God's benevolence?

This discussion probably seems obvious, unless you reflect on the terrible circumstances that force many people to pray. Take a young Kuwaiti woman raped by Iraqi soldiers. Disgraced, her prospects for marriage blown away, her future in tatters, she discovers the ultimate horror: The rape has left her pregnant. What is she to do? How is she to think? Where will she find defenses against despair, against even thoughts of suicide? For her to pray to Allah for help and still say, "as you wish," is a mighty achievement. For her to reach the roots of healing, the green conviction that, despite all that her culture tells her, she has done nothing wrong, she must cross a great desert.

No one can say at the outset whether she will make it. Perhaps it is only even money that her venture in prayer will end with her faith intact. Yet her tradition offers much for her succoring. If the mystery moves her to surrender completely, she can realize, with a great liberation, that only God's judgment matters. Becoming radically religious, she can set Allah against all know-it-all cultural assessments. Carrying her child, braving the scorn of outsiders, she can become the best of all "muslims" ("submitters"), one who obeys despite heavy cost.

What can keep such a woman, or any person asking hard questions and favors, going? A moment of peace now and then. The mystery remains dependable. Life never becomes so obvious that the judgments of outsiders, the mores of one's culture, seem infallible. Always there are chinks, valid reasons for further questions. From time to time we can escape through them. From time to time we can realize, in our own language, on our own terms, that One alone is God. The judgments of societies easily become idols. For Islam, idolatry is the great sin. So the very harshness, the so obvious injustice, of the social scorn directed toward the raped woman tells her volumes about Allah. With God things must be different. Otherwise, Allah is no God, just another tyrant.

The same for people asking relief from other tyrants. Addiction, sickness, marital failure, mental breakdown—all can swell up into idols. In praying to escape them, and submitting oneself to God "as you will," we immediately put them within borders. Not even cocaine can define me. Cancer is not my middle name. Though I have botched two marriages, my life remains mysterious. Though my mind has cracked from strain, I may still have a meaning, some purpose some day to be revealed.

This escape from idolatry, this entry into further possibilities, flows directly from "as you will." When "as you will" follows our prayers as a suffix, the mystery takes breath in our souls. We do not know what we are asking. We vote to endure an adventure. Living or dying, succeeding or failing, gaining or losing, we make God responsible for our final fate. After we have done what lies within our power, we cede to God the judgment on our work. No one else can make this judgment. No boss or priest or even voice in our own head has the authority. If we have asked God, the divine mystery, for what most ails us, whether we end up healed and whole depends on God. We are free of the final responsibility. Our task is limited to what we can do. We cannot guarantee our own sufficient meaning, cannot lay on our own heavenly health. All that depends on a meaningful universe, which only divinity can guarantee.

ANSWERS

I tend to think that any outcome of prayer that enables us to keep going is a positive answer. This view dovetails with my commitment to giving the divine mystery a blank check. The mystery is never failing. It is there when I leave in the morning, there when I return at night. More times than not its presence is pregnant, suggestive, positive, supportive. More times than not I intuit in it a third dimension, the chance that life may be "more." Depending on this third dimension, this possibility of a "more" that is fuller life, I find extremely helpful letting the mystery feed me my life day by day. Whatever happens becomes a matter to take to it for review. I ask the mystery for what I think I need, adding "as you wish." Then we get together to pore over what has happened.

Suppose, for example, that I have asked for help with the myeloma threatening my marrow. If it is good, let the cancer be contained, recede, ideally go away. My doctor and I are doing our share. He is plotting the chemotherapeutical strategy. I am popping the pills or offering my arm to the needles. After the first go-round, when sufficient time has elapsed to check for results, we find that the aberrant protein spike indicating the presence of myeloma has fallen from 5.0 to 2.3. After the second chemotherapy, it has fallen further, to 1.7. Thus electrophoresis suggests that the incidence of myeloma has contracted to only about one third of what it was when we started. Consequently, we may speak of a remission, partial and probably temporary but nonetheless encouraging. Has God answered my prayers (and/or those of others with better claims upon him)?

Why not—but also, who can say for sure? Things are moving as I have petitioned. For the moment I am regaining some of my health. Presently, it seems that God wants me around for a while, though precisely why I cannot say. Emotionally, spiritually, I find it good to be grateful. Thankful feels like the right state of soul. I have reason to bless the divine mystery because, as Hannah and Mary sang in their famous biblical songs, my Lord has done great things for me. It *is* a great thing to have had one's life drawn up from the pit, even if the pit should soon reclaim it. It *does* take one's breath away to have been saved, hauled back from the yawning abyss. Should one stay mute about such a favor, sit there obtusely like a dummy? I think not. I think it would be wrong not to take my remission as a smile of God, a token burnished lovingly. I think it would be churlish to doubt that God has acted, answered my plea with wholesome bread. If only on the level of mental health, I do well to comport myself as a believer.

However, suppose that six months from now things change. I, my wife, and our friends continue to ask God to restore my health, extend the remission and healing, but the aberrant protein spike changes. The line of the graph begins to ascend again, moving back through the twos and entering the threes. Is God no longer answering my prayers? Ought I now to feel abandoned? If my Muslim *in-shallah,* "as God wills," has been genuine and not bogus, I have to reply carefully.

God may be answering in terms I cannot fathom. My true good may be something I cannot currently see, would not now choose. I do not have to say that the resurgence of myeloma is a good thing. I need not utter the absurd words that cancer is not a physical evil, is something we should accept rather than fight tooth and nail. But I have to say that cancer, like everything else in my life, is finally more than I can appreciate. I have to allow that, in the strange ways of divine providence, cancer may be for my final destiny no less a good than health.

Does this mean that I have made God unfalsifiable—the great sin that simple moral logicians fear? It does indeed. When dealing with the divine mystery, sojourning in the wilds of prayer, we end up living well beyond logic. At our wits' end what is most reasonable is what most helps us survive. If it keeps us sane to write the mystery a blank check, we should take out our book and start scribbling. We need not say that we are willing to equate sickness with health, that we have become lovers of failure and pain, or that we understand why life should often turn cruciform. Indeed, we should never speak anything but the strict truth, never deny any outrage or anger welling up within us. But we should bow low before the divine mystery. We should keep ever before our faces the utterly objective foundation for our "as you wish."

None of us can ever say with complete certitude what is for our ultimate good and what is bound to defeat us. All of us who are trying to be radically honest have to say that much always depends on our dispositions—what we make of the apparent good or evil that befalls us. I believe that God is answering us whenever with God we can make what befalls us bearable, even enlightening. I believe that as long as the future remains open, as long as our lives still bear us the possibility of meaning, beauty, and love, we have not been abandoned. We are still on track for heaven. We may still dream of eternal life.

FAITH

Much that I have said about granting the divine mystery a blank check, dealing with the ever-present darkness as an always-possible source of meaning, amounts to a description of living by faith. As noted, students of the basic needs of the human spirit have often found faith requisite. Long before the apostle Paul, Heraclitus realized that reason could not be taken narrowly, had to stretch to match the full bend of the spirit round the corner of what is experientially certain, toward the depth of the mystery and the uncertainty of the future. The just person lives by faith, because the just person realizes that life is mysterious. In simple honesty, that is the way our lives parse. There is always more than we can fathom. In nature, other people, even ourselves, we keep coming upon surprises. Only the dull find new days boring. The alert sense that the mystery is always playing around. Play, mystery, play. Give us new songs, new sacraments, new beauties to rivet us.

In trouble, we find our faith threatened. It is hard to trust other people, when they have let us down time after time. It is hard to trust ourselves, when again and again we've rubbed our faces in our weakness. And it is hard to trust God, pray to God, when our need meets only silence. Until we've learned to frame our petitions with "as you wish," and this frame seems right rather than pietistic, our faith in the mystery will not be supple. We'll creak and crack rather than move easily. We'll lack the grace of the children of God.

We can help form our spirits to faith by pushing ourselves to be positive. We can call on beauty in nature and other people to give us things to celebrate. Why should there be this beauty, when we see how easily ugliness spawns? What does this beauty counsel, when we taste it in the leisure of contemplation? If there is a mystery of evil, a great surd hanging over all the disorder in the world, there is also a mystery of goodness and beauty. If cancer is a primal stumbling block, a scandal over which we're bound to take a tumble, so is good health. Think of all that needs to go right for your cardiovascular system to function without error for twenty-four hours. Think of what is involved in swimming one hundred laps. Why should we assume that our bodily systems have come with seamless warranties? Is it not amazing that for fifty-two years my bone marrow did not clone protein aberrantly?

I do not say that thoughts such as these justify faith in God. The only adequate justification for faith in God is finding that living by it is vivifying. Faith is much like a love affair. We grow in love only by trusting our beloved. We learn deeper mysteries, intuit greater beauties, sense greater wonders, only by believing we will not be misled. And if we can do this with fallible human partners, patching things up with ramshackle forgiveness as need arises, we can do it globally, entrusting ourselves to God's mystery. The darkness will never desert us, nor will it always be oppressive. The gamble of faith is that most days it will carry us. The hope of faith is that now and then it will bear us up on eagles' wings.

HOPE

Does hope lie within our power? In urging it, am I not risking blaming the victim, asking the down-and-out for more than they can rustle up? These are penetrating questions. As our book-length inquiry ends, it becomes clear that trouble has many levels. We want to solve the practical problems threatening to overwhelm us: finding the money for rent, getting the children into day-care. More deeply, we want to gain control of our emotions, feel we have some say over our lives. Most deeply, though perhaps less aware, we want to come to grips with our constant fragility—why we die and how we may live even though always imperiled. I think that sufficient hope to struggle to survive is a function of ordinary physical and mental health. If we have not broken down, we have enough hope to search for the rent, work at finding a day-care center. Beyond this minimal hope, though, I suspect we need help if we are to hope more broadly.

By now the possible sources of such help stand well surveyed: friends, professional counselors, teachers, books, and much more. Any that make a contribution are precious, and we should take their aid gratefully. Still, in this book I have been drawn remorselessly into the resources of one's own spirit. The encounter with life's mystery in prayer has impressed me more and more as the crucial meeting ground. And there I see that no one else can do my worrying, my suffering, my dying for me. No one else can convince me I have good reason to go on. I cannot alienate my life, expect another to construct my character. If I do not find faith, hope, and love within me, I shall never get out of my trouble.

Often when I've taught undergraduates, I've found them resisting this analysis. We begin with a story of trouble. They are intrigued to follow it onto deeper ground. But they rebel when they start seeing the implications. They do not want to take hold of their own spirits, become responsible for their own view of life. The idea that how they think might determine what they become is very frightening.

Certainly, I agree with them that a Buddhist scripture such as the *Dhammapada* has its limitations. I concede that famine and flood, like cancer and crime, work along whether we like it or not. But I'm appalled that they won't face the requirements of their own humanity. Why can't I make them see that, until they are willing to think reflectively, they are bound to remain superficial? It seems to me obvious that remaining superficial is a great source of trouble. If we lack depth, any breeze can blow us away. Indeed, my whole argument here has been that we can outlast many of our troubles, if we build on rock rather than sand. The mystery is my rock and my salvation. Thus I would always have you build on it.

I can hope to become a millionaire, but how significant would that be? I can also hope to become a person whose life makes sense, even though a dozen dangers threaten it. I believe this latter achievement would be significant. Yes, a million dollars can shape a life and influence many others. But a way of looking at time that engages us with its unfailing mystery can take us beyond our emotional troubles. We cannot hope to avoid death, even to avoid sore suffering, by accumulating a million dollars. If we look at our time correctly, we can hope to reconcile ourselves to death and prepare ourselves for suffering. We can hope to put order in our souls. I believe that such order has a strong overflow onto our other troubles. I am convinced that if my students would abide in the desert, learn about contemplation and self-criticism, they might enter upon the promised land: peace and satisfaction. But I cannot force them to this, as I cannot compel you, gentle readers. Common observation suggests that few Americans apprentice themselves to reflection willingly. Most are dragged into it by trouble.

If so, notice how paradoxical hope usually is. Neither students nor any others are ever hopeless. Anyone can muster the courage to be and to confront all inner demons. But chances are that x or y will not do this until he or she is suffering. Thus the best hope for x or y to become reflective, more than superficial, is for him or her to stub a toe, turn an ankle, pull a hamstring. This is a curious situation, perhaps one providential. Wisdom comes through suffering. The true dimensions of life appear when we are faced with death. We appreciate saints only when we've been slashed by sinners. We gasp at the wonders of the mystery only when it emerges from nothingness.

In other words, if you hope to escape your troubles, your best ally is the spiritual state those troubles themselves spotlight. The more directly you walk into your mind-set, confront your fears and obsessions, own up to your limitations, the quicker you'll see what's involved. The trouble itself barely matters. It can be drugs or divorce or drinking, parents or children or spouse. If it is your trouble, it has set itself up in your spirit. Only as you learn how it got there, what it is doing there, and how you can exorcise it will you gradually overcome it.

Each step of the way the mystery can help you. Each effort to learn and let go can increase your strength. That is why the spiritual life, any effort to understand and change, is so hopeful. That is how hope becomes synonymous with simply trying.

LOVE

The mystery we face in prayer presents us the bare fact that we exist, that there is a world, that something has triumphed over nothing. What might explain this bare fact, this positive tether? Well, what gives rise to life? What is the most obvious source of creativity? Is there a single word by which to name the divine mystery, indicate the obvious source? I believe there is. I call the mystery love. The world that I experience makes most sense if a limitless love holds it in being.

The world continues to exist, despite entropy and other signs that it could slide into nothingness.

Human beings continue to reproduce themselves, despite all the hatreds of history. And most people continue to struggle after meaning, to resist physical and spiritual death, even though much around them suggests their struggles are foolish. Something in both the world and ourselves remains romantic. Something refuses to take the grimmer, easier option and drop out. Something stays bemused by life and light, beauty and possibility. It is hard to exaggerate its importance.

One sees this something regularly in parents. Nothing in the bargain they strike when begetting and raising children proves they are reasonable to take so much trouble. What keeps the majority going far exceeds common sense. For love of their children, parents work for decades, take great care, and often keep their mouths shut. Half-aware, the children pay them back with a winsome smile. The parents seldom complain bitterly. Somehow they know the children will settle the debt by caring for the next generation. And so it keeps going on, a love affair with being, continuity, increasing and multiplying—a love affair that makes little sense apart from the mystery. Even hurt, disappointed, broken apart, human beings still tend to keep trying. What is it they are trying? What is it we are seeking, longing for, using to keep ourselves going even when we're troubled?

To my mind, it is clearly love. Pleasure, power,

possessions, flattery—all empty very quickly. Yes, they can keep trivial people in thrall for many years, but no person of substance regards them highly. No, the only treasure befitting our hearts is the love that comes as a miracle. The only force stronger than death is the yes that gives us ourselves with full worth. We cannot compel this yes from others. We cannot find it for sure in the natural world. Yet it hovers on the divine mystery like a constant breeze. To deal with God is to contend with a lover.

This is as true when we are pained as when things are easy. In pain, afraid for our lives or our peace or our happiness, we react as though abandoned. Life, the mystery, God, our own assumptions, have let us down. We did not expect to be dumped into trouble. We feel in every bone that it's simply not right. We ought to be loved and cherished. We ought to feel protected and lovable. The great threat in trouble is that it may make us feel unlovable. The salvation in feeling loved is that it restores our possible worth. When the mystery returns roundly, positively, so that even our sickness or financial disaster turns out not to be a dead end, our worth is still possible. Until there is no mystery, we may still find the love that could save us.

Naturally, we need worth, and so love, to keep on living. We have to think we justify all the trouble. When we no longer feel we do justify all the trouble, we come into genuine spiritual peril. So if we could think that the mystery itself justified us—that the being of God made us worthwhile—we could speak of truly profound salvation. And if this justification by the mystery were its own loving, a function of the mystery's freely wishing us well, we could say that our worth stood outside all this-worldly peril. For then the simple fact of the mystery would make us safe, freed, lovable—because in fact loved.

I cannot say how persuasive any given reader will find this musing. It is the end of a lengthy rumination, gone far deeper than I initially expected. Perhaps on good days nearly everything I've suggested will seem at least plausible. Perhaps on bad days most will seem but empty noise, sound and fury signifying nothing. If so, then you of course must decide. Are your good days more indicative than your bad days? Is it better to hunker down with minimal hopes or let yourself soar?

I have no guarantees with which to bribe you. At the end, as at the beginning and constantly throughout, the final significance of your troubles lies between you and the mystery. What do you find this day, when you present your grievances to the mystery? How on this night does its silence resound? It is reward enough for me to have primed you to hear these questions. What you answer in your heart of hearts can remain all your own. I only urge you not to fear to make your answer, and to love it in the measure it comes from the mystery of your trouble.

CONCLUSION

The Method Summarized

OUR QUESTION HAS BEEN, HOW CAN WE BETTER handle the troubles that afflict us? My answer has been, By taking stock of our inner resources—specifically, our precisely human capacities for thinking, feeling, sharing, deciding, and praying. In conclusion, let me summarize briefly some practical approaches to mastering each of these capacities.

First, you can get on top of your thinking. You can learn how your mind tends to operate. If you pay attention, you can recognize your need for information, how you can sharpen your understanding, what good judgments require. Your mind is your constant equipment. The better you can deploy it, the more success you are likely to have in handling your troubles. So push yourself to master your mind. Tell yourself it is ignoble for human beings not to know how to use well the faculty that makes them human. Set out to become a person who is reasonable—guided by what is so, not what is desirable or would be lovely. To be reasonable is not to be cold or rationalistic, only to be hard on your own illusions, fantasies, self-indulgences. Many of our troubles come from our being foolish. Most of our troubles diminish when we take our minds in hand.

Second, you can become intimate with your own patterns of feeling. If you pay attention to your emotions, your moods, your consolations and desolations, you can learn how beauty and danger tend to move you. Look at your grossest fears and the most delicate of your hopes. Make them come out of the closet and report to you. What keeps you from going back to school, confronting your overbearing boss, getting rid of your feckless boyfriend? Why do you keep showing up late, never pay your bills on time, remain unable to balance a checkbook? Clearly there are things you are fleeing. Obviously there are sides of yourself you are unwilling to face. What is the pain you are avoiding? Why would you rather stay numb than deal with your depression? Our feelings are our equipment for maneuvering through the world of values—what we esteem, and what we depreciate. The better you can steer with this equipment, the more able you will be to skirt emotional troubles and establish yourself in peace.

Third, there is help available all around you. You need only reach out, open up your innards, ask others in to share what's troubling you. It is not good for human beings to squat alone in the darkness. Trouble shared is trouble halved. The more intentionally you set out to obtain help by sharing, the clearer your gains are likely to be. So take aim at your friends, at congenial members of your family, at counselors ready to help. Resolve to break out of your isolation and let a breeze of objectivity blow in. Other people are a great source of perspective. When their impressions create a regular pattern, your troubles will fall into much better focus. Then you will be able to compare how you think and feel with the reactions of outsiders, people more detached and so probably more realistic. Then you will be able to realize that you are not the only one with serious problems. Any sharing is bound to show you that trouble thrives on every corridor. It is good for you to recall this. It is bad for you to feel singular, unique, persecuted. So share what is happening to you. Think that talking with others, creating emotional ties to others, is natural and right.

Fourth, you can challenge yourself to do things about your troubles. Having learned about your thoughts, feelings, and friends, you can make yourself face up to necessary decisions. The moment comes when one has to fish or cut bait. You can prepare for this moment and so see it as necessary, even desirable. To keep spinning your wheels is sickening. At some point mental health will require your bailing out or committing yourself to remain in, your taking a stand one way or another. You can't keep giving your dysfunctional child money that she uses to hurt herself. You can't keep putting off firing the employee who has proved untrustworthy. So look hard at what goes into a good decision. Inform yourself well about how to move from judgment to action. Consider carefully what wise people say about peace and tranquillity. Then do it: Gird your loins and make a move.

Fifth and last, the depths of your personality, the roots of your thinking, feeling, sharing, and deciding, invite you to prayer. The mystery holding all your significance, perhaps especially that of your troubles, solicits a response. How are you going to deal with never being certain precisely what your life means? What are you going to do about death, failure, injustice—all the harsh realities that weave in and out of human troubles? On the other hand, what about little children, beautiful days, the miracle of being loved without merit? How ought these gracious realities to color your sense of your troubles? You have to deal with these deeper issues. Until you do, your spiritual life is half-baked. My counsel is that you hand yourself over to the never-failing mystery. I believe you will handle your troubles best when you feel your life is a gift of love. So I think that the praying that praises the mystery, calls it divine, feels it to be loving, and asks it for sustenance relativizes any trouble.

For people who pray, any trouble is both shared and submitted to a horizon of limitless creativity. Thenceforth, it becomes legitimate to believe, hope, and love far beyond strictly human potential. Our troubles, like our selves, engage us with transcendence—a mystery greater than the world of space and time, a mystery suggesting eternal life. No one can ratify this mystery for you, but if you find it through prayer, you'll feel freed once and for all. No trouble will tyrannize you any longer. Not even death will write your finis. So you would be as foolish not to pray as not to study your thinking or feeling. You would be as dumb and cowardly. You can never get away from the mystery. Always you are wise to open your heart to it, share your pain with it, make it your measure and Lord.

Suggestions for Further Reading

Appleton, George, ed. *The Oxford Book of Prayer*. New York: Oxford University Press, 1985. A good selection of prayers from the world religions.

Barry, William A. *Now Choose Life*. New York: Paulist, 1992. A Christian approach to change of heart and renewal.

Borysenko, Joan. *Minding the Body, Mending the Mind*. New York: Bantam, 1988. Psychology and relaxation techniques in the service of both physical and mental health.

Coles, Robert. *The Spiritual Life of Children*. Boston: Houghton Mifflin, 1990. Psychological, medical, and religious perspectives on the struggles of children for growth and meaning.

Frank, Arthur. *At the Will of the Body*. Boston: Houghton Mifflin, 1991. Reflections on illness rooted in experiences of heart disease and cancer.

Leavitt, David. *Equal Affections*. New York: Weidenfelt & Nicholson, 1989. A fine novel of a dysfunctional family challenged by homosexuality and cancer.

Levine, Stephen. *Healing into Life and Death*. Garden City, N.Y.: Doubleday/Anchor, 1987. Eastern spirituality in the service of both physical and mental healing.

Merton, Thomas. *Thomas Merton: Spiritual Master*. Edited by Lawrence S. Cunningham. New York: Paulist, 1992. An excellent collection of major writings of a recent Christian guru.

Mitchell, Stephen, ed. *The Enlightened Heart*. New York: Harper & Row, 1989. A good selection of poetry from spiritual masters of the world religions.

Stoddard, Sandol. *The Hospice Movement*, rev. ed. New York: Vintage, 1992. A challenging exposition of the history and philosophy of an alternative, holistic system of health care.

Suzuki, Shunry. *Zen Mind, Beginner's Mind*. New York: Weatherhill, 1970. Conferences of a Soto Zen Master that offer much aid toward peace of soul.